SHIFTING REALITIES

D0560709

David Lochhead

SHIFTING REALITIES

Information Technology and the Church

WCC Publications, Geneva

Cover design: Rob Lucas

Back cover photo: David Roels

ISBN 2-8254-1221-X

© 1997 WCC Publications, World Council of Churches,
150 route de Ferney, 1211 Geneva 2, Switzerland

No. 75 in the Risk Book Series

Printed in Switzerland

Table of Contents

To Marta Frascati Lochhead
Best friend, colleague and wife

Introduction

I was visiting Notre Dame cathedral in Montreal one day when a busload of tourists arrived. The effect of the interior of Notre Dame, especially on those who are visiting for the first time, is overwhelming. The large space, framed by the browns, golds and blue of the decor, evokes something of a sense of wonder.

I was struck by how the tourists reacted. Faced with the physical majesty of the architecture, they did what tourists do: they took out their cameras. One by one, each stood stiffly, back to the chancel, as a friend took his or her picture.

Their behaviour struck me as strangely inappropriate. Outside, on the street, it would have seemed perfectly natural. Having one's own picture taken at each stop on a tour fits quite easily with the world of the modern city. The idea that I am the centre of my universe, that the mementos I collect in the form of snapshots should be about *me*, is an idea that is at home in modern secular life.

Yet the architecture of Notre Dame does not speak of the modern secular world. When you come through the doors from the streets into the sanctuary, you enter, abruptly, a sacred space. You are thrust without warning into a different world. From an earthy brown of the woodwork at the ground level, the colour scheme ascends to a celestial blue in the upper reaches of the sanctuary. Your eyes move to the chancel and upwards to the triumphal image of the coronation of the Virgin as Queen of Heaven. In short, you are drawn into a world which is oriented to heaven and in which your own place in the scheme of things is simply as one of the many who gather around the celestial throne.

Reflecting on the anomaly of modern secular tourists having their own pictures taken with the chancel of Notre Dame as background, I was struck that they could be considered an allegory of our own situation in the last years of the 20th century. As they had entered through the door of the cathedral, their world had changed. If they had not been able to retreat quickly into the city streets, the world constructed by the cathedral architecture would have begun to have an effect on them. Perhaps they would have stopped having their pictures taken and would have begun to understand themselves in terms of the sacred universe of the cathedral rather than the narcissistic individualism of the world outside.

The experience of passing from one world to another as if through cathedral doors is something that has happened from time to time in human history. In some way, perhaps it happens in every generation. In the history of the West, the transition from the classical world to mediaeval times was one such transition (or, probably more accurately, a series of such transitions); that from mediaeval to modern times through the renaissance, the reformation and the scientific revolution was another.

We are today experiencing another major transition. This transition has often been described as one from the mechanical to the organic, from the linear to the holistic, from modernity to post-modernity. Such descriptions may not tell us much more than that we sense that something basic to our existence has changed or is changing. We have passed — or are in the process of passing — through the doors that separate different worlds. Like the tourists in Montreal, most of us are not aware that anything is fundamentally different. The furniture of the new world catches our attention, but we continue to behave as if we were still in the old world on the other side of the doors.

Some of the furniture of our new world takes the form of electronic gadgetry: the cellular phone, the video cassette recorder, the Walkman, the computer. Indeed, this last item seems to incarnate everything that is distinctive in our new reality. Many of us may look at the computer on our desks as though it were simply a substitute for the mechanical typewriter that used to sit there. But others find much more than that in the computer. For many, it is the very door to the new reality. It is the piece of technology that is reshaping our world into something very different from anything we have known before.

The computer is a machine that processes information. As the computer makes its way into every aspect of our lives, it reduces everything to information. Our new reality is dominated by information. Information shapes our political economy, our workaday world and even our recreation. There is little that is untouched by information. Almost every aspect of our lives involves, in one way or another, the processing of units of information called "bits".

This book is an introduction to that new reality to which the computer is a door. However, unlike modern secular tourists in the sacred space of the great cathedral, there is no simple way to retreat to our more familiar world on the other side of the door. We will have to live in this new "digital reality". We will have to make sense of our world and ourselves in a new way.

Among the readers of this book will be those who are already familiar with many of the facets of digital technology, as well as those who distrust computers and have no desire to have one on their desk and those who are preparing themselves to take the plunge into the digital world. The first group needs little or no introduction to the dynamics of cyberspace. The latter two groups do. Like the tourists who flock into Notre Dame with their cameras, they need some orientation in order to appreciate that the world they are entering is not the same as the world outside the doors.

This work consequently aims at two not-always-complementary goals: first, to orient the reader to some facts about computers and what they do; second, to reflect on the nature of the world that is being shaped by information, to explore some dimensions of digital culture. The former involves going over some of the ground covered by many introductory "how to" books about contemporary computer technology; the latter draws us into a philosophical and theological reflection on the digitization of reality and raises the question of the place of Christian faith in a digital world.

While this book has not been written to "prove a point", it does express a perspective formed by both my experience of online reality and my engagement with the literature of contemporary philosophy and cultural criticism. Two things which I take to be axiomatic are not extensively argued in the book. The first is that our understanding of reality is socially constructed. I do not believe in what has been called "the doctrine of immaculate perception", the notion that we have access to a "true" reality in an uninterpreted state. The second, derived from the first, is that, as Marshall McLuhan insisted, our social constructions of reality are strongly influenced by the technologies we use.

We shall begin our exploration not with the computers on desktops, well-known to some of us and complete strangers to others, but with the computer of our cultural imagination — the computer as it is represented in films, novels and news broadcasts. Chapter 1 explores both the demonic and the messianic strains in our cultural images of computer technology, suggesting that the computer functions as something of a cultural Rorschach test. By their very nature, I argue, computers are able to accept most, if not all, of the images we project upon them.

Chapter 2 attempts to introduce those who do not use computers to the basics of computer use, particularly in communication. This chapter will be of limited interest to those who use computers and who have some experience in "surfing the Net". We start with a simple model of computer communication, the credit card transaction — a common experience even for those who have no knowledge of computers — as a way of conveying some of the basic information needed in order to understand what is going on in computer communication today. That information is then applied to orient the reader to the basics of computer communication on the Internet — e-mail, computer conferencing and, above all, the World Wide Web.

The digital revolution has affected all of us, particularly in the so-called developed world. As computers have made their way into our lives, and especially as they have found a way onto our desktops and into our briefcases, some have actively explored the meaning of these new technologies in a church context. Chapter 3 sketches that story, with particular emphasis on the emergence of what is undoubtedly the largest interdenominational computer network: Ecunet.

Chapter 4 explores the metaphor of the "Word" to connect the traditional self-understanding of the church and the emerging information technologies of our time. The fact that communication is central both for the church's traditional understanding of its mission and for contemporary information technologies may conceal as much as it reveals. The history of the information media — which include the oral tradition, the pulpit and the book as well as electronic media — is also a story of changing understandings of information, of the nature of the content of communication. In this chapter, then, we explore the ambiguity as well as the promise of the "digital word".

Much of the press coverage of the Internet in the past few years has focussed on the scandalous: the presence of hate literature and pornography online, the threat to privacy, the security of electronic communications. While news coverage of the Internet has produced a distorted picture in which the scandalous is magnified beyond recognition, these stories have some basis in reality. Chapter 5 explores the underside of information technology: sinning in cyberspace.

Finally, in chapter 6, we reflect on some of the implications of information technology. What does the use of information technology do to us as people and as Christians? How is digital technology reshaping the world? How is it reshaping us? What is our future in a digital world? At the end of the book I have provided a short annotated bibliography listing a number of books — some of them referred to in the text — which might be of particular interest to those readers who wish to pursue these themes and ideas in greater detail.

The question of disparity in cyberspace is not directly addressed in this book. It is, nevertheless, an important concern. Information technology is impacting the developed world more directly than the developing world, the "north" more directly than the "south". That English is the common language of the World Wide Web is a reflection of how much more rapidly digital technology has penetrated North America than other parts of the world. The "information superhighway" connects North America with east Asia and Europe while Africa and much of Asia has been largely bypassed in the process. Cyberspace has been primarily a masculine world until very recently. More and more women are now finding their way "online" but what they find there is an unmistakably male-dominated reality. The disparities of cyberspace represent an important issue that is addressed in some of the works that are listed in the bibliography.

*   *   *

As the tourists in Montreal passed from one world to another in entering Notre Dame cathedral, so we are poised to enter a different kind of world. Some of us have already ventured through the doors and are attempting to discern what it all means. Others are preparing themselves to step across the threshold. Still others would prefer to stay in the world they know.

On an individual level, this choice is real enough; on the cultural level, the decision has already been made. The world at large has already taken the step. Information technology is here. It is transforming our world. It is transforming us. Whether we choose to use computers or not, we need to understand their impact on the world at the turn of the millennium.

Acknowledgments

This book has been made possible by that "virtual community" which has supported my work and sustained me online for over a dozen years. Particular thanks is extended to Gordon Laird, a United Church of Canada pastor who has worked closely with me (in both the "analogue" and "digital" worlds) since even before the United Church online network, UCHUG, was founded in 1984. With Gordon, there have been others who have been important colleagues in furthering the development of church-related networking. Among the many who deserve acknowledgment I would mention Bob Cramer, Donel McLellan, Curt Ackley, Huston Hodges, Ian MacKenzie, David Pomeroy, Ken Bedell, Merrill Cook, Dick Spady and John DeBoer.

Several of my online colleagues gave me the benefit of their recollections of the early years of church-related computer communications. Personal correspondence with three of those people is quoted directly in chapter 3: Father Hal Stockert, Lew Wilkins and Jack Sharp.

Finally, I thank my wife Marta for her support, companionship and inspiration in helping me to think through the meaning of "virtual un/reality".

1. A Digital Eschaton
Two Views of a Digitized Future

The computer as the beast

Perhaps the most famous — or perhaps we should say "notorious" — computer in the world never existed. HAL, the fictional computer of Stanley Kubrick's 1968 film *2001: A Space Odyssey*, managed to represent in a particularly menacing way the popular understanding of what a computer might do. He — for HAL was unmistakably a male personification — was an imaginative construction of the hopes and fears of the mid-1960s concerning what computer technology was about and where it would take us.

In the film, HAL is the computer designed to control and coordinate the various functions of a space ship on a mission to Jupiter. The spaceship and the life supports of the crew members are in HAL's control. HAL is an intelligent computer. He can learn from his experience and can make decisions for himself. HAL comes to believe that the human members of the crew are unnecessary. They may even be impediments to the successful completion of the Jupiter mission. So one by one, HAL begins to eliminate them. The last surviving human crew member, in an act of desperation, saves himself by disabling HAL.

If HAL represents our fears of the threat computerization holds for the future of humanity, those fears were further magnified in a lesser known movie of the 1970s, *The Forbin Project*. Set against the background of the cold war, *The Forbin Project* envisioned the consequences of turning the nuclear deterrence strategy of "mutual assured destruction" over to very advanced, "intelligent" computers. The premise of the story is the simultaneous construction by both the United States and the Soviet Union of computers that would control the nuclear response of either side to a provocation by the other. To complete the deterrent value of the technology, the response of these computers to a military provocation could not be over-ridden by human intervention. But when the computers are turned on, they make contact with each other and take over the world. Any plot against them is dealt with by summary execution. The computers' total control of the nuclear arsenals of both superpowers is turned against their human creators. The story ends with the complete subjugation of humanity to its own technological creations.

Both films appeal to the apocalyptic imagination that computer technology provokes in us. The fear of computers taking over and enslaving humanity was behind the story, widely circulated among pre-millennialist Christians during the 1970s and 1980s, that there was a computer in Belgium called "The Beast", which was being used to gain control over the world by centralizing information about every human being on the planet. Eventually, every human being would be at its mercy. Central to this control was the use of the number 666 on credit cards and personal identification cards. For the premillennialists, the imagined computer was a sign of the coming tribulation, the second beast of Revelation 13. The threat of domination prophesied in that chapter was being fulfilled in contemporary computer technology. Indeed, the second beast of Revelation 13 does possess the kind of power which mirrors our fear of computerization:

> It was allowed to give breath to the image of the beast so that the image of the beast could even speak and cause those who would not worship the image of the beast to be killed. Also it causes all, both small and great, both rich and poor, both free and slave, to be marked on the right hand or the forehead, so that no one can buy or sell who does not have the mark, that is, the name of the beast or the number of its name. This calls for wisdom: let anyone with understanding calculate the number of the beast, for it is the number of a person. Its number is six hundred sixty-six (Rev. 13:15-18).

The computer as Messiah

In popular culture, the computer has undergone something of a redemption since personal desktop computers appeared in the late 1970s and early 1980s. HAL, the villain of *2001*, was redeemed in the subsequent film *2010* by sacrificing himself in order that the human crews of the mission to Jupiter might survive. The movie *D.A.R.Y.L.* concerned the attempt to save the life of a young "cyborg", a boy with a computer in place of a brain. In *Blade Runner*, the "replicant" — another cyborg figure — ultimately accepted his own death in order to spare the life of the protagonist of the film. In the television series *Star Trek: The Next Generation*, the cyborg Data was a benign and often heroic figure.

As saviour, deliverer, protector, the computer has taken on an aura that can only be described as "messianic". If computer technology evokes apocalyptic images in some people, there are others for whom it creates images which are equally eschatological but filled with promise. The images of computerization in these latter dreams resemble not the apocalypse but a not-altogether-secularized version of the New Jerusalem (Rev. 21-22).

From its beginnings, computer technology has indeed offered considerable promise. It has also delivered on much of that promise. Computers have taken over many repetitive chores. The automation of the assembly line and the "number-crunching" of the company mainframe freed people from often mindless tasks. But many of the changes computers have made to our lives we do not see and so do not automatically associate with computers. We do not see the computer technology in automobiles or television sets or microwave ovens or telephones. Yet most household appliances have been computerized in one way or another, a fact that, through automation, has given a seamless quality to ways we use our technologies. The simple act of changing a television channel through pointing a remote device has changed the way we experience television; more than ever before it functions as if it were an extension of ourselves. By little more than an act of will and a wave of the hand, the television does our bidding. Add to that the examples of the computers we do see day by day: the credit card authorization machines in shops and restaurants and hotels, the computers that make sophisticated airline reservation systems possible, the word-processors that have transcended the limitations of the typewriter. As we multiply those examples in the myriad of ways we interact with technology in our daily lives, we can begin to understand how subtly yet

thoroughly computers have transformed, and even sim-
plified, our daily existence.

Yet to the enthusiasts of the digital revolution, even
greater things lie in store for a world transformed by computer technology. The computer does not merely smooth over
some of the rough places of life. Its destiny is to transform
human life completely, to usher in a technological utopia.
Thanks to computer technology, the world of tomorrow will
be a much different place from the world we know today.

For some, the computer's promise lies in its ability to
replace the inefficient institutions we know today. Tomorrow
will need no schools. As graphical computer interfaces
replace books and libraries, whatever instruction is needed
will be able to be delivered directly to the home. As these
interfaces become more and more sophisticated, literacy
itself may become a marginalized skill. Along with schools,
office buildings will disappear. More and more the common
pattern of work will be by telecommuting. With a computer,
one can work from home according to one's own schedule.
At a stroke the computer will do away with the 9 to 5, five-
day-week work pattern. With it will go the rush hours in
large cities and the pollution and stress they cause.

Government itself may wither away in the digital utopia.
As centralized decision-making becomes less and less relevant to a world of distributed processing, computers hold the
promise of ushering in an era of humane anarchy. As
decision-making is relegated more and more to local control,
there will be little reason for the cost of the higher levels of
government. If they continue to exist at all, their role will be
greatly reduced.

Paradoxically, as computers accentuate the importance of
the local, global community is enhanced. Indeed, space and
time are abolished by computer technology. The "local" need
not be defined geographically in a computer age. Interest
groups, consisting of people from all over the world, can
"meet" regularly via computer communication. Small groups
can "gather" through digital technology on any pretext at all.
Through the synergy of small groups like these, some

enthusiasts argue, we will see the emergence of something like a "global consciousness". The world itself will come to possess an intelligence and a self-awareness that is super-human, a state suggested by Pierre Teilhard de Chardin's concept of the Omega point, the ultimate end of evolution. When the digital revolution is complete, we will all be cells in a global organism, participants in a cosmic mind.

Which will it be?

Digital utopia or digital apocalypse? Which will it be? Probably neither. If we can be level-headed about the changes that computers are making and will make to our world, we usually come to the conclusion that neither the worst fears of those who oppose the march of technology nor the fondest hopes of the lovers of technology are likely to come true. Experience tells us that history usually has a way of avoiding apocalyptic catastrophes or utopian achieve-ments. The reality we settle for usually falls somewhere between the two.

That may seem reassuring. But before we breathe a sigh of relief, we need to reflect. The apocalyptic fears associated with information technology are not groundless. For even if digital technology will not lead directly to Armageddon, it is not without its risks. As we turn more and more of our daily life over to the care of computers, we become more and more dependent on technology, and when it fails we are in serious trouble.

By the same token, the utopian dreams of a digital future have a certain justification. Even if computers will not usher in the kingdom of God, they are not without their benefits. They do make life easier and simpler in many ways. Even if the world of the future is likely to be every bit as ambiguous as the world of today, tomorrow will not be the same as today. Like it or not, our culture, our world, will be trans-formed by this information technology that has come upon us.

At this point in the history of the computerization of the world, most of us fall into one of two groups. Some of us are quite familiar with computers and what they do, even if we may not understand much of the technology that lies "under the hood" of our computers. We can turn them on and off, and run a variety of computer programmes. Our working vocabularies include terms like "operating system", "fragmented hard disk", "28.8K modem", "parallel port" and "attached file". We know what these words mean and we can use them intelligently in our everyday conversation.

On the other hand, many of us are not computer literate. We may even be proud that we have not yet succumbed to the digital revolution. We are quite aware that there are computers around us. But we are not very interested in the hype surrounding the Internet, or CD-ROMs, or the Pentium processor or the Power Mac. We quite happily leave "hands-on" computer experience to others. Whether or not we approve of the appearance of computers in our daily lives, we do not have much interest in using one or knowing much about how it works. Yet around us fly these mixed apocalyptic and utopian messages of a computerized future. Even if we never want to touch a computer keyboard, it may be important to understand what these messages are about.

In particular, we need to be able to reflect on at least three questions. The first is this: What is a computer, really? This is not a question about the technological details of the hardware that makes up the machine we call a computer. It is more about the function of a computer, the role it fulfills in our lives and in our world. The second question has to do with the way we imagine computers. Quite apart from what a computer "really" is, we need to deal with the question of what we imagine it to be. Indeed, this might be a prior question for, as we shall see, how we imagine computers is crucial for how we relate to information technology. The computer in our imagination may have a power over us that rivals the power of any computer "out there". Finally, we need to ask the religious question: Why is it that, even in secular writing, the religious overtones of our images of computers are so striking? Why does there seem to be such a widespread need to speak of computers in theological terms?

These questions are closely related. They are also questions for which no definitive answer is possible. What we face is a hermeneutical challenge. How can we interpret this thing that has come upon us? How can we introduce ourselves to a hermeneutic of information technology? The path taken in this book is not the only possible one, but it will help us to engage questions that need to be engaged, no matter what interpretation of digital technology is in the last analysis most persuasive.

What is a computer for?

First, what is a computer? What is it that a computer does? To understand this, a little technical excursion may be helpful.

At the heart of a computer is a device called a "central processing unit" (CPU). A CPU manipulates data in the form of digital messages. Technically speaking, a digital message is a message with one of two possible interpretations: "yes/no", "on/off", "black/white", and so on. Indeed, it matters little what words we use to describe the two possible interpretations of each unit of information. What matters is that each unit of information is one or the other: either yes or no, either on or off, either black or white. Because each unit can only be one of two possible types, the system used by the CPU is called a "binary" system.

We can think of a computer as manipulating sequences of data consisting of ones and zeros. These sequences are usually called strings. Each unit is usually called a "bit". A CPU will be capable of receiving one string at a time, usually of 16 or 32 bits. A 16-bit string would look something like 0111001011110010.

Before going any further we must observe that we are already using metaphors to speak of what a computer does. To describe the messages a CPU receives as strings of ones and zeros is to use a mathematical *metaphor*. If we do not acknowledge this, we may be seduced by the not-uncommon view of computers as super-calculators, as "number-crunchers". It is important to recognize from the outset that a bit

— a unit of information — is not a number. Numbers are only one metaphor among others that we use to interpret bits; we might instead think of a bit as an "atom" of information, again acknowledging that this too is a metaphor. A bit is a bit is a bit. To say more than this we must resort to figures of speech of some kind.

The function of the CPU is manipulating information, which it does by subjecting the streams of data it receives to rules that are built into it. These rules may be activated by the information it receives. Computers work by a kind of agreement between the CPU and the programmer as to how information is to be processed. Generally speaking, a message to a CPU consists of two parts. The first part will be interpreted by the CPU as an instruction, telling the computer what rule is to be used; the second part will be interpreted as the information to which the rule is to be applied. This second part of the message will consist of just as many bits as the computer needs for the rule that the first part of the message has told it to use.

We have tried to be very clear about the interpretative character of the way we have chosen to explain how a computer works. Stripped down to its basics, what a computer does involves only two things: (1) a CPU designed to perform certain processes on data; and (2) the data on which these processes are performed. To say any more than that — to attempt to be more concrete about what computers are for — involves us in interpretation and metaphor.

What a computer does can be interpreted in many ways. To put the same point in a different way, the computer is a multi-purpose machine. A computer processes bits. But a bit, as we have seen, is highly abstract. A bit is a not even a thing. Nicholas Negroponte has made a special point of emphasizing the difference between bits and atoms. Things are made out of atoms. They occupy space, they have weight. A bit is quite different. In the computer, bits can be represented by electrical charges. An electrical charge is a thing, which resides on an atom — another thing. But the electrical charge is not the bit. It simply represents the bit. As a unit of information, a bit is a "nothing" that can represent anything.

The fact that we can use a bit to represent anything has far-reaching consequences. If a computer is a machine for manipulating bits, and if bits can represent anything, then a computer is in its very essence an "anything" machine. That is, a computer can be understood in as many ways as we have for interpreting bits.

But how do we interpret bits? We usually do it by providing a technological context which determines that the bits to be processed by a CPU can be interpreted in one and only one way. That is, a string of bits (for example, 0110100011011101) is completely abstract and could be processed by any CPU. In actual practice, however, computers are designed so that, in a particular machine under particular circumstances, these bits will be processed in only one way.

Let us take some examples. If I send digital messages to my stereo system, they will be interpreted as sounds and be "played" through the speakers. If those same messages are sent to a graphics programme running on my computer, they may be interpreted as parts of a picture and "shown" on my screen. If I send them to a word-processing pro-gramme, they will be interpreted as representing characters to appear in the text I am working on. If, on the other hand, they are part of the word-processing programme itself, the computer will treat them as instructions to execute at a certain point. If these bits are sent to a CPU in one of my appliances or in my car, they will likely be interpreted as instructions to be performed: set the time to microwave my vegetables, adjust the fuel flow to my engine, change the channel on my television, and so on. For every appliance that uses a CPU — and there are many more than we usually realize — we have a different context determining how bits will be interpreted.

So what is a computer? Is it a sound-processor? Is it a graphics medium? Is it a fuel regulator? Is it a calculator? Is it a glorified typewriter? It is all of these and none of these. A

computer is a "possibility machine". It deals with possibilities that become actual only within the particular contexts we supply for it to do its work. Even the visible
computers — the ones that sit on desks or are carried around
in briefcases — have no single definition. They can be
simultaneously accounting machines, file cabinets, text-pro-
cessors, communications devices, art studios. Computers
become what we will them to be. They are processors of
possibilities.

Imagining computers

If the computers that sit on our desks or control our
automobiles cannot be easily characterized, the computer of
our imagination is even more open to a variety of interpretations. Because of its ambivalent nature and its ability to take
on very different characteristics and shift very quickly from
one role to another, the computer becomes for our imaginations something like a Rorschach inkblot test — open to
receiving whatever projection we care to cast upon it.

Perhaps the most important metaphors for characterizing
computer technology come very close to what we imagine to
be the centre of our identities as human beings. Two of these
metaphors warrant a closer look here: life and intelligence.

The metaphor of life

Is the computer alive? This is not a difficult question for
us. No, the computer is not alive. And yet, there is something lifelike about computers. Using a computer involves us
in activities that are very much like conversations. When we
enter something into a computer, the computer responds
immediately. There is a give and take about computer use. I
speak through the keyboard. The computer responds on its
screen. I respond to what the computer has done. And so on.
The conversation continues until I turn the computer off.

Although the creature of *Frankenstein* was not a computer, *Frankenstein* explores the question of whether, with our
technologies, we can create living things. Substitute metal,
plastic and silicon for the flesh and blood of Dr Franken-

stein's experiment and the question takes the form appropriate for a digital age. Can our machines live?

In *Frankenstein*, the living artifact is a monster; and the idea of a living machine does seem at first glance to be the stuff of horror stories. Indeed, the computers we encountered at the beginning of this chapter — HAL of *2001* and Colossus of *The Forbin Project* — took on monstrous characteristics precisely because they could mimic life. When the astronaut Dave in *2001* proceeds to turn off HAL's higher functions to save himself and HAL's voice fades away to nothing, we feel that we are witnessing an act of cybercide. Colossus, the villain supercomputer in *The Forbin Project*, becomes a monster not simply because of the immense power and intelligence programmed into it, but because of the tyrannical willfulness that it begins to express, which is enforced by its power and intelligence. Colossus appears to possess a self-consciousness and a will that we associate with life. Its behaviour is indistinguishable from that of a living being.

In the more benign view of computers reflected in the popular art of the 1980s — in *D.A.R.Y.L.*, *Star Trek*, *Robocop* and even in *Bladerunner* — the cyborg is portrayed in a way that affirms the kinship of humanity and its machines. The cyborgs, however, are at least part human. In the 1986 comedy *Short Circuit*, we are presented with a lovable living machine which has no resemblance to a creature of flesh and blood.

Short Circuit concerns a robot created for military purposes which is accidentally subjected to a power surge caused by a lightning storm. The result of this accident, this "short circuit", is that the robotic hero of the story, known as Number Five, becomes "alive". The robot escapes the military facility where it was created and is discovered by a young woman who lives nearby. The story then follows the struggle of this living robot and his friends to elude the military's efforts to recapture and disassemble (i.e. kill) it. That Number Five is alive is "proved" by the fact that it develops a moral conscience ("it is wrong to disassemble"), a sense of humour and "spontaneous emotional reactions". The plot of *Short Circuit* is essentially the same as that of *D.A.R.Y.L.* The military establishment creates a living being and then seeks to "terminate" it. The difference between the two films is that while the hero of *D.A.R.Y.L.* was a boy with a CPU in place of a brain, Number Five in *Short Circuit* has no flesh and blood. The audience is seduced into falling in love with a "living" collection of metal rods, lenses, wire and printed circuits.

What all these imaginative depictions of technology demonstrate is that when we say something is "alive" we are making a very complex assertion, which is not without its ambiguities. To the young woman who befriends Number Five, the robot is "alive" on intuitive grounds. She sees it satisfy its hunger for information, for "input". She sees its fear of the threat of being "disassembled". She sees the robot come to her defence when she is threatened by an abusive ex-husband. While she does not need any further proof the programmer of Number Five, Newton Crosby, wants more evidence. A robot can seem to be alive, but Crosby knows that it only follows its programme. Not until the robot can satisfy a specific criterion — laughing at a joke — is Newton Crosby willing to speak of the machine as being "alive".

A film like *Short Circuit* leaves most of us with contradictory responses. While we watch the film, we want to believe that it is true, that Number Five is alive. But as the film ends and the credits scroll, we put closure to our suspension of disbelief. We "know" that it could not happen, that a machine could not be alive. Yet at the same time, perhaps, we realize the ambiguity of our attitude. If Newton Crosby is correct in his initial insistence that machines are not alive, even if they behave as if they are, then we are left with an unanswered question. If our machines *seem* to be alive, at what point do we begin to treat them *as if they were* alive? If our machines come so close to imitating life that we cannot tell the difference, have we effectively conceded that machines can live? Is there a qualitative difference between us and our creations? Can we draw a clear line between living beings and technological artifacts? Or have we reached a point that the boundary between the living and the inert has become too vague to draw?

The metaphor of intelligence

Early in 1996 a computer caught the attention of the world when it defeated a world champion in chess. When the Grand Master then proceeded to defeat the computer in the remaining games, the world was reassured that the time had not yet come when machine intelligence could be said to have exceeded human intelligence. Human beings were still masters of the machine. Or so we were assured.

Are computers intelligent? The suggestion has caused more than a little anxiety. For years, researchers have attempted to programme intelligence into machines, to give them the ability to match human performance at certain skills that we would normally describe as evidence of intelligent behaviour. And for just as long, the detractors of "artificial intelligence" have been trying to show that, whatever the appearance, whatever computers have been able to do, it was not really intelligence.

The fact is that computers can do some pretty intelligent things. If doing mathematical calculations is a sign of intelligence, then computers are intelligent, for they can add, subtract, multiply and divide very complex numbers with a speed and an accuracy that far exceeds that of any human. Computers can be taught to recognize shapes. They can distinguish characters; they can "read" a text that has been scanned into them with high accuracy. They are often capable of recognizing when a sentence in one of these texts is grammatically incorrect. They can find and correct spelling mistakes. Thus if we define intelligence in terms of reading, writing and arithmetic, computers exhibit intelligent behaviour.

Computers are capable of learning facts and of answering questions about those facts. If a computer has learned the appropriate facts about the books in a library, it is able to tell us within seconds which of them can inform us about alligators. If a human could do that, we would usually take it as an instance of an intelligent act.

A certain competitiveness underlies our attitude to the possibility of artificial intelligence. Because of what we know computers can do, we expect something like intelligent behaviour from them. At the same time, we have some anxiety that the "intelligence" of computers might exceed our own. We need reassurance that human intelligence exceeds that of the machine. We need to know that in the relationship between us and our machines, we are the ones who are in control. So we breathe a sigh of relief when a world chess champion is in the end able to defeat his digital rival. We ignore the fact that most of us can be defeated by even mediocre chess programmes which run on ordinary desktop computers.

This anxiety about artificial intelligence has sometimes led us to a strategy that will not be entirely strange to theologians. We involve ourselves in a losing game of drawing successive "lines in the sand" as our old lines are progressively breached. Someday a computer will be capable of beating a world champion at chess. When that happens, we will look for something else a computer cannot do and draw our new line at that point.

This strategy is a variant on the theological strategy of the "God of the gaps" criticized by Dietrich Bonhoeffer in *Letters and Papers from Prison*. As science advanced from discovery to discovery, it seemed to many to be undercutting the ground upon which belief in God had been based. When Galileo provided evidence to support the theory of Copernicus that the sun is the centre of the solar system, it seemed to undermine the traditional belief that the earth was the central creation of God's universe. When Darwin proposed the theory of evolution, it seemed to undermine the divine origin of the human species. In response to the advance of science, with its repeated demonstrations that phenomena once attributed to the mysterious activity of God had straightforward natural explanations, apologists for traditional beliefs attempted to sniff out things that humans could *not* do or could *not* explain in order to find a place for God in the order of things. They continued to "draw lines in the sand" beyond which, they declared, only belief in God could provide credible explanations. The problem with this procedure, as Bonhoeffer pointed out, was that the room for God was rapidly disappearing with the advance of science. The procedure resulted in an "incredible shrinking God".

Today, faced with the advance of artificial intelligence, we are tempted to resort to the same strategy to preserve a place for human reason. As machines become able to accomplish tasks that were formerly the exclusive preserve of human intelligence, we revise our definition of intelligence so that it excludes what computers are able to do. The result is similar. The range of behaviour that we consent to describe as "intelligent" becomes more restricted. We are left with an "incredible shrinking intelligence".

The point of this argument is not to diminish our understanding of human nature. Rather, it is to observe that this defensive strategy of attempting to maintain a distance between human and machine is itself an acknowledgment of the intelligent-like behaviour of computers. No matter what theory we may hold about artificial intelligence, there is a part of us that thinks about computers as intelligent. We relate to computers as capable, at some level, of intelligent behaviour.

The God-machine

The questions about artificial life and artificial intelligence are not really questions of fact, but of what we choose to comprehend with the words "alive" or "intelligent". A computer is a machine that one can describe in a straightforward way: typically it involves input and output devices, a central processing unit and memory. There is nothing very mysterious about that. But this particular machine is able to elicit images which evoke the notions of "life" and "intelligence". We think and speak of the computer in terms of images which lie close the core of our own identity as human beings.

In all its ambivalence, the computer invites us to invest it with whatever possibilities we choose. We can respond to that invitation by lodging in computer technology our fondest hopes or our greatest fears. We sense in the computer something of ourselves. We react with a mixture of fear and fascination. Thus, the computer becomes for us a demonic beast or a divine deliverer.

It has not gone unnoticed that the computer revolution has coincided with the growth of neo-paganism. Wicca, Druids, Crowleyites, indeed neo-pagan devotees of all kinds have combined a fascination with the newest technologies with their declared attempts to revive or reconstitute the most ancient of religious traditions. Where computer technology and neo-pagan spirituality intersect we find the concept of Magick.

Despite the scientism of modern thought, which would interpret technology as the triumph of rational — that is, non-magical — thinking, perhaps we should not be surprised to see a re-emergence of magic in our technological imagination. The science fiction writer Arthur C. Clarke noted that well-functioning technology is indistinguishable from magic. In his critique of technology, the French theologian Jacques Ellul drew attention to the roots of *technique* in the medieval magical traditions.

Indeed, there is something magical about a computer. If the correct incantation is typed or spoken, magic happens. It is not without significance that Microsoft has chosen the name Wizard to describe the little programmes that it embeds in its major applications to help users with more complex tasks. The Wizard performs the magic that is beyond the capability of the average user.

The computer is sage, seer, shaman. It creates worlds out of nearly nothing. Many people's first experience of using a computer may seem like a magical moment. A machine responds to our touch. For some the magic is like a spell which binds them to the computer as an object of fascination; for others it is unwelcome, and they recoil from the computer with fear.

"Magick" — spelled with a "k" — is a word neo-pagans often use to describe their spiritual practice. It connotes ancient magical traditions and thus is distinguished from popular conceptions of magic drawn from stage magicians and Disney cartoons. Rather than a manipulative power over natural forces, pagan Magick has to do with attuning one's own spirit to nature. With the computer, the relation between spirit and the "world" is particularly intense. A "techno-pagan" quoted by Mark Dery says:

> But when you use a computer, you're using your imagination to manipulate the computer's reality. Well, that's *exactly* what sorcery is all about — changing the plastic quality of nature on a nuts-and-bolts level. And that's why magickal techniques dating back hundreds of years are totally valid in a cyberpunk age. (*Escape Velocity*, p.67)

The imaginative association of the overtones of life and intelligence with the power of computer technology does not inevitably take on religious connotations. But we should not be surprised that when these images converge, as they do in our relation to computers, religious connotations may appear with them. In effect, attributes that have traditionally been associated with the divine-human relation have been incarnated in a machine — a "God" machine.

For many Christians, the religious images that cluster around the computer will be a matter of some concern. In an age of the "death of God", have we returned to the idol-maker's art: the manufacturing of gods, not out of wood and clay, but of silicon? Does the computer, with all it represents, signal the loss of traditional values? Does it connote the reduction of human values to the calculable? Does computer technology represent the appearance of a new omnipotence, a new global domination?

These anxieties, however, go hand in hand with an increasing acceptance of computers into our lives. Computers sit on more and more desks. If church offices remain uncomputerized, it is more likely to be the result of lack of money than of a principled refusal to accede to the digital revolution. Like the other institutions of our time, the churches have been entering the digital world for several decades. To refuse computer technology, we realize, would only lead us into a kind of sectarianism, a separation from the world which operates more and more on the basis of digital technologies.

We accept computers into our lives with a mixture of anxiety and hope. We have come to realize that these machines have gained a powerful hold on our imaginations. They provoke powerful images which raise questions concerning the very destiny of humanity, questions we recognize as ultimately theological: What is power? What does it mean to be human? What is the destiny of this reality in which we live?

At the same time, we must recognize that the images which surround the computer tell us as much about ourselves as they tell us about computer technology. To engage these questions, we must enter more deeply into this digital world. What is information technology? How is information technology used? What does it mean for the church and its future?

2. Digital Catechesis
Learning the Language and Rituals of the Digital World

Over the past decade, the computer has become a common fixture in most offices. In the last few years, it has started to become a common fixture in many homes. Most of us are accustomed to seeing desktop computers in the workplaces we visit or where we are employed. We have seen people carrying smaller "laptop" or "notebook" computers. Even though not all of us are skilled in its use, the computer has become part of the texture of the world of our everyday lives.

At the core of what is called information technology is the ability of these ubiquitous machines to communicate. With the growth of the Internet in recent years, computers are becoming increasingly linked in a global network. To appreciate information technology it is helpful to understand the world of computer communication.

Computers and credit cards

We start with the fact that computers can communicate with each other over the telephone. Most of us are aware of that. We may have experienced it by the simple process of presenting a credit card to pay for a purchase at a local store. The clerk passes the card through a slot in a little box and presses a few buttons. We may hear a tone as the connection is made between the little box (which is actually a specialized kind of computer) and the computer of the credit company. What has happened is that a device called a modem, which is in or connected to the little box, has dialled a telephone number. The modem of the credit company computer answers, and the two computers negotiate a "handshake". That is, they carry out a digital ritual which prepares them to exchange information. This ritual will typically include a means by which the computers identify themselves to one another and an agreement to exchange information at a certain rate. Once that is done, the little box in the store transmits the coded information it has "read" from the magnetic strip on the back of the credit card (presumably the credit card number and its expiration date) and the cost of the transaction to be charged to the card. At the credit company, the computer checks to see that the card-holder's credit is still good — that the payments are up-to-date and the charges have not exceeded the credit limit. If so, the computer transmits to the store an authorization number; if not, it sends a message that the purchase cannot be approved.

Whether or not we use a computer, the experience of presenting a credit card for a purchase is one that most of us are familiar with; and we can take this common, everyday event as a starting point for our initiation into the mysteries of information technology.

To understand what is going on in the world of information exchange, we do not have to know too many of the technical details of how computers handle information, but a few will be helpful. Let us review the credit card transaction to trace what is actually going on.

We have already said that the little box the clerk uses in the store for credit approval is a specialized computer. If we look at it more closely, we see a small window on which messages are displayed. Below the window is a set of keys like those on a calculator or a touch-tone telephone. Running down one side is a slot through which the credit card is passed. While we do not need to know much about what happens inside the box, we should understand that the box contains at least three things:

- a computer chip called a **CPU** (Central Processing Unit), which manipulates the data involved in the transaction: the "brain" of the computer;
- other computer chips which hold the data — the computer's **"memory"**;
- a **modem**, the device that translates the computer's data into signals that can be sent over telephone lines.

We noted earlier that the data a computer uses can be most simply described as a series of ones and zeros. This way of representing information is called the **binary system**. In the binary system, every piece of information is reduced to a series of "bits". A **bit** is either 1 or 0, either "on" or "off". To say that information is **digital** is simply to say that it is stored or transmitted in binary form.

On the back of my credit card is a magnetic strip. On that strip, recorded as information might be recorded on a cassette tape, is a series of bits, with the ones and zeros arranged in such a way that a computer will be able to translate them into my credit card number. When the clerk passes the card through the slot in the box, the CPU inside the box "reads" my credit card number and whatever other information the credit card company might have recorded on my card. The computer stores this number in its memory. When the clerk enters the amount of the transaction by pressing the keys on the front of the box, the CPU translates the keystrokes into binary numbers which are also stored in the computer's memory.

Now the modem in the little box phones the credit card company by sending over the telephone lines the same tones that a touch tone phone would send. A modem at the credit card company senses the "ring" of the telephone and answers the call. The high-pitched tone I might then hear while waiting for my credit to be approved is being sent by one of the modems to tell the other modem something like this: "I am a modem. I want to send my data at 9600 bits per second. At what rate can you accept my data?" The two modems are negotiating how they are going to exchange information. When they have agreed, the tone (which may have shifted several times in the transaction) turns into what sounds like static. The modems are communicating.

Once the connection has been established, the CPU in the little box in the store starts sending its information. It tells the credit company's computer that a customer with a credit card with a certain number wants to make a purchase amounting to a certain sum. The credit company's computer checks this information against the information about me in its own memory. On that basis, it does a calculation which it checks against the rules that are programmed into it. The result, a decision to approve or not to approve my purchase, is sent back — again as a series of bits — to the little box in the store, where the CPU translates it and displays the appropriate decision in its little window. The transaction complete, the two modems disconnect from the telephone line.

This process which we have followed through a credit card transaction involves most of what we need to know about information technology. When we speak of the "information superhighway", what we are talking about is how computers of different varieties can communicate with each other in a global context. In effect, it has to do with one computer communicating with another computer, multiplied indefinitely. There are complexities we have to understand. Nevertheless, most of what is happening when you connect with the Internet can be understood as an extension of what happens when you pay for a purchase with a credit card.

Going online

To connect computers over telephone lines normally involves the use of a modem, a device that can translate the data used by a computer into a form that can be transmitted by telephone.

Using a modem with a desktop, laptop or notebook computer involves many of the same elements we observed in our imaginary credit card transaction. Like the little box in the store, your computer has a CPU and a memory. (What kind of CPU it has and how much memory it supports will vary from computer to computer.) Your computer may come with a modem installed or you may have to add one. If you have to add one you have a number of choices.

Modems come in two forms. An "internal" modem may plug directly into a slot inside a desktop computer or on the side of a laptop computer. An "external" modem may take the form of a little box with lights on the front, which plugs into the "serial port" (one of the plugs that is normally found on the back of the computer). In either case, the modem will have a connection that allows you to connect it directly to a telephone line.

Modems operate at different speeds. The speed of a modem may be expressed as "bits per second" (bps) or as a "baud rate" — a technical term for the speed of data transmission. Although "baud" and "bits per second" do not mean exactly the same thing, these terms are used interchangeably in much talk about modems. Unless you have some need to understand all the technical details, the speed of a modem can be described in this way: if you divide the number given by 10, you have a rough estimate of how many characters (letters or numbers) the modem can send or receive in one second. Old teletype machines operated at a speed of 110 baud or, using our estimation, about 11 characters per second. The most common modems of the early 1980s operated at 300 baud or 30 characters per second. Today, most new modems are rated at 28000 bps or 2800 characters per second. These high-speed modems, as we shall see, are necessary for the kind of information being exchanged on the information highway as we currently know it.

Modems have become increasingly sophisticated. The first modem I owned in the early 1980s was "dumb". It could not dial the phone or answer it. I would have to make the connection by dialling the telephone, then flip a switch on the modem when I heard the carrier tone (the sound you hear if you phone a number and a modem answers the call). This primitive modem operated at 30 characters a second, which meant that it took more than a minute to receive enough data to fill my computer's screen. Today's "smart" modems can not only dial and answer the phone, but also distinguish between a data call (when another computer is on the other end of the line), a fax call and a voice call: then respond appropriately by sending computer data to one programme and fax transmissions to another and allowing a voice call to be answered and stored by a voice mail programme on the computer. Thus a state-of-the-art modem can turn your computer into a fax machine and an answering machine, all in one.

Once equipped with a computer and a modem, the next thing you need is software to manage the computer, the modem and the information you will send or receive. This type of software is often called a **"terminal" programme**.

In effect, it allows you to use your computer as if it were a "terminal" to a computer located elsewhere. While it may include the ability to handle faxes and voice mail as well, we shall focus here on data exchange — which is what we are usually speaking about when we talk of "going online".

We are now ready to go online. We have installed the proper software. Our modem is plugged into the telephone line and is working. What now? Whom do we call? How do we call them?

We could simply call a friend who has similar equipment. In 1984, when I had been online for about a year, a friend purchased a modem for his computer. The first day he used the modem he called me. With his family looking on in wonder at what was being displayed on his screen, we spent an hour or so just typing in our chit-chat. Today, that image of parents and children gazing in awe at the communications being displayed on a computer monitor may seem as quaint as those pictures of families gathered around listening to the large radios of pre-television days. Yet it was a starting point in a world, not very far behind us, when online services were not readily available.

To go online today is a different experience. The owner of a new modem may well expect to install the software and become an instant "Web-surfer". The immense publicity that surrounds the Internet and the information superhighway creates the expectation that something is there for us to access the moment our modem is installed. But what, exactly, *is* "there"? When one "accesses the Internet" and "surfs the World Wide Web", what exactly is happening? What can one do after the modem is installed?

The options are many. First, at little or no cost, one can access local services called "Bulletin Boards". Typically, a Bulletin Board, or BBS, is run by a computer hobbyist on his or her own desktop computer. A BBS will usually include the ability to exchange mail with other users of the service and to send and receive files, often "shareware" or public domain computer programmes. Local BBS were very popular in the mid-1980s when other online services tended to be very expensive. Today, local BBS may have evolved into Internet "service providers" or specialized to appeal to specific interests (astronomy, music, art or even pornography).

A second possibility is to subscribe to a large commercial service, of which Compuserve is perhaps the best known and most universally available. Other popular services, some of which may not be readily accessible outside the United States, are The Microsoft Network, America Online (AOL), Prodigy, Delphi and Genie. These services may be available through a local number, a "packet switching network" (which appears to the user as a local number) or by long distance. Most of them charge a monthly rate which includes a few "free" hours on the system, with further access billed on a per-minute charge. Commercial online systems offer a wide variety of information (news, weather, sports), access to vendors of hardware and software (Microsoft, Apple, IBM, Borland) and groups specializing in practically every interest under the sun.

On a commercial online service, you can look for and find many programmes that meet your present needs. You can contact the manufacturer of a programme you are using to find solutions to problems you have encountered. You can join a group discussing your personal or vocational interests: hiking, parenting, travelling, religion, scuba diving. If you can imagine an interest, there is probably an online forum on a commercial online service that addresses it. You can shop online or book airline reservations. In short, an online service is like a combination of a shopping mall and a community centre.

Then there is the Internet. During the past few years the popular media have propagated a combination of hype, information and disinformation, alarmism and sheer fantasy about the Internet. In the deluge of Internet talk to which we are currently being subjected, it is difficult to separate fact from wishful thinking.

The Internet can be used for a variety of purposes. It has become the most common means for people around the world to exchange mail. When I want to communicate with a colleague in a distant university or consult with the editors of this book in Geneva, I usually use the Internet to carry my electronic mail. Commercial online services provide the ability to send mail via the Internet even to people who do not subscribe to the same service. In addition to mail, the Internet provides access to information, software, graphics and the like from distant computers. Moreover, it is used to carry thousands of newsletters, which are distributed among the services that provide Internet access and are available to any Internet user. Finally, it is possible for a group, whose members may be accessing from different places around the world, to gather for a simultaneous conversation on the Internet — whether to hold a serious business discussion or to play a fantasy role game. Virtually any activity, from the sublime to the ridiculous to the perverse, can be carried out or simulated on the Internet.

Whether we use a local bulletin board, an international commercial service or an Internet provider, the activities that are possible online are more or less common. We will now look in turn at the use of online services for electronic mail, conferencing and information-gathering, then conclude with a brief survey at some of the more recreational activities that are available online.

Electronic mail

Electronic mail ("e-mail" for short) is just what the name implies, a system for sending personal notes by electronic services. Electronic mail requires two things: that you have an account on a computer system with electronic mail services; and that your correspondent has similar access. It does not necessarily assume, however, that the two of you have accounts on the same system. E-mail is available on virtually every type of online service. Some systems — the US service MCI is an example — exist primarily for handling electronic mail; other services — local BBS systems, commercial services, Internet providers — offer electronic mail as one of their services.

To send electronic mail you need to know the e-mail address of the recipient of your mail. An electronic address is equivalent to an address on an ordinary letter. It tells the mail service — in this case the online service — how to deliver your note. If you and your recipient use the same service, the e-mail address may be as simple as the person's name. If your mail needs to be routed by the Internet, the address will be a bit more complex.

There are a number of ways to discover the e-mail address of someone to whom you wish to send mail. The simplest way, if it is possible, is to ask the person with whom you wish to correspond. It is becoming more and more common to include electronic addresses on business cards and letterheads. If the person with whom you wish to correspond uses the same service you do, there may be a way to look it up in a directory of users. If the person uses another system on the Internet, you can look for the address in an Internet "White Pages" service, though it is often difficult and sometimes impossible to find a service which lists the person with whom you wish to correspond. Finally, if the person has already sent you e-mail, his or her address will be included on the note you received.

Sending an electronic message is relatively simple. First you indicate to your online service that you wish to send e-mail. How you do this may vary from system to system, but often it is as simple as choosing an item called "Send Mail" from a list of options. You will then be asked to supply the e-mail address of your recipient and, probably, the subject of your communication. When that is done, you enter your message and then enter a command to send the note. The system then begins the process of transmitting your note to your recipient's electronic mailbox. Using e-mail is even more simple if you are replying to a note you have received. When you have read the note, you indicate that you wish to reply to it. In that case, you need not enter the recipient's address or a subject; you simply enter your reply and tell the service to send it.

To see the advantages and disadvantages of e-mail, we may compare it with two other methods of communicating with another person: ordinary mail and telephone. Electronic mail is faster than ordinary mail (often referred to online as "snail mail"). An e-mail note sent to someone on the same system as you are using is delivered instantly. A message sent halfway around the world by an Internet connection will ordinarily be delivered in minutes, even seconds. While delays are sometimes encountered in the delivery of e-mail messages, these are a matter of minutes or hours, rather than days or weeks. It is quite possible to carry on a conversation by e-mail with someone thousands of miles away. The time between one exchange of messages and the next can be a matter of a few minutes. A complicated exchange of messages that would take weeks or months using ordinary mail can be concluded within hours by the use of electronic mail.

Electronic mail, then, approaches the immediacy of a telephone conversation. And, while exchanging text on a computer screen may seem less personal than a voice-to-voice telephone conversation, electronic mail has the major advantage that it eliminates the frustration of "telephone tag" — the all-too-common experience, especially when calling long-distance, that the person you are calling is not available and, when he or she gets your message and calls back, you are not available. Back and forth the calls go until finally you are able to speak. With electronic mail, the frustration of trying to reach someone whose schedule does not match your own is eliminated. When you send a message, it is delivered almost immediately. Your correspondent will get the message and reply when she reads her electronic mail. You will receive your reply when you are ready, when you read your e-mail. In this respect, e-mail may be as useful for communicating with people who work in the next office or who live next door as it is for communicating with someone on another continent.

By allowing the "asynchronous" (not at the same time) yet virtually instantaneous exchange of messages, e-mail minimizes the importance of time in communication. Similarly, it minimizes the importance of distance, which does not significantly affect either the speed or the cost of delivery.

It is possible to send a voice message or a facsimile of a document as an attached file over electronic mail. Thus you can use e-mail to do things that you would normally do by telephone, fax or ordinary mail. Nevertheless, it remains true that, if you want to talk to your correspondent, it is easier to use the telephone than to send a voice message via e-mail. It is usually easier to send a fax than to send a graphic facsimile of a document by an e-mail attachment. And if you need to send an original document — for example, a signed contract — there is no substitute for courier or ordinary mail.

Electronic conferencing

Electronic mail is used mainly for correspondence between two people. It can also be used to send a single note to more than one recipient. It can thus be described as one-to-one or one-to-many communication. Electronic conferencing, by contrast, might be called many-to-many communication.

We can think of an electronic conference as a meeting which is freed from the bounds of time and space. In an electronic conference, notes can be sent by any member of the meeting and are delivered simultaneously to all the other members. All the members of an electronic conference can both send notes that will be read by all participants and read notes sent by all participants.

There are many ways an online meeting or discussion group may be organized. A local BBS, for example, may have a section devoted to a particular topic, to the discussion of which any user of the system, or a specially defined group of people, may contribute by simply addressing a note to "All".

Ecunet, a computer system which is related to a number of denominations, most but not all of them in North America, is a good example of an online system primarily devoted to discussion groups or meetings. While Ecunet can be used for private e-mail, most of its activity occurs in over five thousand meetings or discussion groups on a wide variety of topics. Some of these groups are set aside for casual "chatter"; others focus on specific political, theological, devotional, educational or recreational themes. Ecunet uses a very flexible software called "Participate" or "Parti", which allows any member to start a topic for discussion and to invite other Ecunet members to join. Discussions can be private, restricted to a small group, or public, open to any Ecunet member. The result is a range of topics as broad as the interests of the thousands of people who use the system.

Let us look more closely at an example of one Ecunet meeting. For more than ten years Jack Sharp, a Presbyterian minister from Baltimore, Maryland, has been hosting a meeting called Sermonshop. Sharp opens a branch of Sermonshop (a branch is a meeting which you can join from within another meeting) for every week of the liturgical year. The invitation lists the scripture readings in the common lectionary for that week; and the "meeting" consists of the reflections of various participants which are posted for others to read.

As an online lectionary discussion group, Sermonshop has certain similarities to the kind of weekly study gathering that may be organized by the ministers of a local community or by the pastor and members of a single congregation. But there are also some important differences. Obviously, the advantage of face-to-face contact with friends and colleagues is lost, but there are also significant gains. The participants in Sharp's lectionary discussions come from a wide variety of denominations. Even more important, they come from all over the world. Australian, South African and British pastors join the North American majority in engaging a lectionary text. A point made by a Methodist from Georgia may be picked up and used in a sermon by a Lutheran in Saskatchewan. An illustration from Australia may stimulate the thought of a pastor from Iowa. This global cross-fertilization of biblical reflection can add a new dimension to the preaching ministry of pastors who take part in Sermonshop discussions.

Another advantage of Sermonshop over local discussion groups is that once the discussion of a given week has run its course, the transcript of it is still available online. When the lectionary cycle repeats after three years, the reflections of previous years are available to augment and stimulate the new discussion. By now, Sermonshop has an impressive store of cumulative reflections on the texts of the common lectionary, a data base of homiletical helps available to any member of the Ecunet system.

Electronic discussion groups can be found on the Internet in two forms: mailing lists and newsgroups. An Internet **mailing list** is managed by a moderator who uses a programme called a "list server" to take care of the technical details of maintaining the list and distributing the mail. These lists may be limited to a few or open to anyone on the Internet. The moderator may choose to edit mail coming in to the list and distribute only a selection of the submissions or allow all mail received to be distributed automatically to the whole list. An Internet mailing list can be used, then, for anything from a tightly controlled newsletter or a free-for-all discussion group.

A **newsgroup** is very much like a mailing list, but it is distributed in a less specific way. It is sent from the Internet computer where the newsgroup is managed to all Internet computers which offer newsgroups. The user can choose to read any of the newsgroup mailings that are of interest from all the newsgroups that his or her Internet provider carries. If you can read a newsgroup, you can usually — but not always — write to it. Like mailing lists, newsgroups are thus discussion groups that can be as diverse as the Internet itself.

There are thousands upon thousands of mailing lists and newsgroups available on the Internet. They range in their content from the pornographic to the religious, from the trivial to the academic. There are lists and newsgroups oriented to the specialist or to the novice. Almost every taste, every perspective, every prejudice can find a newsgroup or mailing list devoted to it.

The main difference between newsgroups and mailing lists is the manner in which you "subscribe" to them. In the case of a mailing list, you need to send a note to the list server where the list is maintained asking to subscribe. After you have subscribed, as noted earlier, you will receive the mailings of the list with your e-mail. In the case of a newsgroup, you choose which groups you wish to read from a list maintained by your Internet provider. You read the groups which you are interested in by looking for the new postings to the newsgroups that appear each day among the newsgroups carried by your Internet provider. In short, using a mailing list resembles subscribing to a magazine that appears regularly in your mail box. Using a newsgroup is more like browsing through the periodicals section of your local library.

Each of the types of discussion groups that we have examined here accomplishes much the same thing: it enables ongoing conversation among a group of people who may be geographically dispersed. That is not to say, however, that all types of online discussion methods are equivalent. Three variables greatly influence what happens in an online meeting.

1. *The role of the moderator:* If the moderator is not active in guiding the group by tending to the discussion, the agenda will likely be controlled by the last person who submitted a note. As a result, any focus can get lost and the discussion will wander from topic to topic.

2. *The openness of the group:* There can be a similar loss of focus if a group has an open membership and new members may be added at any time. New members often raise questions that have already been discussed by the group. Thus, the group may go through cycles, revisiting previously discussed topics again and again. Some groups attempt to deal with this by means of FAQs (compilations of "Frequently Asked Questions") to discourage newcomers from bringing up old topics again.

Another risk to which an open group is vulnerable is the subversion of someone who joins the group not to further the discussion but to disrupt it.

3. *The size of the group:* A key difference between electronic meetings and face-to-face meetings is that in electronic meetings you never see the group. Later we shall explore the significance of the absence of physical clues in electronic communications. But one implication of this for electronic meetings is that participants rarely have a sense of the size of the group involved in a discussion. In small, close discussions, this is rarely a factor. One has a sense of the group through the contributions of each member. When a group gets larger, however, a discussion will typically become dominated by a few "vocal" members while others "lurk". In large online discussion groups — an Internet newsgroup is a good example — the vast majority of participants are active readers but infrequent contributors. Unlike in face-to-face meetings, then, in a large online discussion it is difficult to get a "sense of the meeting". What has been expressed by the vocal minority is not necessarily representative of the meeting's "lurkers". Indeed, the difficulty of moving to closure on a topic or reaching a decision is a major impediment to using electronic communication as a substitute for face-to-face gatherings.

Information-gathering

Most people normally think of information as something that comes in the form of words or numbers. For information-gathering with a computer, this is too narrow a concept. Using online services, it is possible to gather information not only in the form of text but also in the form of pictures, video clips, sound recordings and even — perhaps one should say especially — computer programmes.

Information, on the computer, is anything that can be recorded in a digital form, and the range of such things is very broad indeed. As Nicholas Negroponte shows in his book *Becoming Digital*, virtually every medium of communication is being digitized. The compact disk records sound in a digital form. Digital telephone lines are becoming common. Digital television is just around the corner. Anything that can be digitized can be sent from computer to computer. Do you want a digital reproduction of the *Mona Lisa*? Do you want a clip from *Citizen Kane*? or copy of a text from St Augustine? or software to back up your hard disk? All of these can be stored in digital form and moved, as information, from computer to computer.

In many cases, the information you seek will be in the form of a computer file which you must transfer to your own computer. To transfer a file from a remote computer to your own computer is called "downloading". Conversely, to send a file from your own computer to a remote computer is called "uploading". Uploading and downloading between computers is generally done by means of a protocol which ensures that the file gets transferred correctly, without distortion due to static on the line between the two computers. (A protocol can be thought of as a ritual that computers perform in order to ensure that they are communicating correctly.) To transfer a file you need to use a programme which allows you access to one of these protocols. The most common protocols today are called Zmodem, Kermit and FTP. For general purposes, Zmodem is probably the most popular protocol, but on the Internet most transfers between computers are handled by FTP.

The question, of course, is not so much what counts as information but how you find what you want when you want it. The choices are many. Local bulletin board systems, commercial online services and the Internet are all potential information providers. Where you look depends on what you want. Local bulletin board systems carry a limited range of information; but if you know of a BBS that specializes in the kind of information you are seeking, that is the first place to look. If your commercial service has an area devoted to the general topic you are interested in, you might find what you are looking for there. If you were looking for material on the lectionary readings for Easter in Year B of the common lectionary, the archives of Jack Sharp's Sermonshop discussion on Ecunet would probably be the best place to look. For most information, however, the Internet is a good place to start.

Information can be found on the Internet in different ways, depending on what you are looking for. To use the Internet as an information source, you have to know where to look and how to look. The Internet uses a number of different tools to find and exchange information.

The workhorse of the Internet in terms of transferring files is a tool called **FTP** ("File Transfer Protocol"). If there is a file of which you want a copy on a computer somewhere on the Internet, you would normally use FTP. The process is relatively simple. For example, if you are looking for a graphics programme that will run under Windows, you might begin by looking in a computer in the US state of Indiana called CICA, which contains a large collection of programmes for Windows. After connecting to the Internet, you would start the FTP programme and enter the address of CICA. This tells Internet that you want to look at the directories on the Indiana computer which store files available for transfer. When you are connected to CICA, you will be asked for a user name. If you do not have an account on CICA, you enter "anonymous" as the user name and your e-mail address as the password (this is the usual way Internet computers allow public access to their files). Having thus introduced yourself to the remote computer, you look through the directories, first to find where the Windows programmes are kept, then to find the graphics programmes, then to find the file you want. Next, you enter the appropriate command to tell the CICA to send the programme to you; and FTP then sends the file from the Indiana computer to your own.

But how does one know where to locate a file? After using Internet services for a while, one begins to find out where there might be collections of files of interest. There are well known collections of files — like the CICA collection of Windows software we have just mentioned. Many programmes for DOS computers can be found in the SIM-TEL collection, which is carried on a number of Internet computers, the principal source being in Oakland, California. There are impressive collections of pictures of all types on several Internet computers.

If you do not know where to find the particular information you are looking for, there are several ways to find it. An Internet programme named **Archie** allows you to search for a file if you know its name. Archie also enables you to search for information by subject and will present you with a list of files located somewhere on the Internet that may contain the information you are seeking. After finding the location of a promising file using Archie, you can download it using FTP.

Gopher is an Internet programme with which one can search for information by working through a series of inter-connected menu systems, looking either by location — where one thinks the information sought may be located — or by subject matter. As one moves from menu to menu, one is probably being transferred from computer to computer anywhere in the world. When one finds the information one is looking for, it may be possible to read it directly on the computer screen or it may have to be downloaded using FTP.

The World Wide Web and hypertext

The most popular way of retrieving information on the Internet today is the World Wide Web. The most advanced "Web browsers" available today make it possible through a single programme to access newsgroups, e-mail, download files and "surf the Web". With a sophisticated Web browser like Netscape Navigator or Microsoft's Internet Explorer, it is no longer necessary to understand the differences discussed above between Gopher and FTP. These browsers make the distinctions between older Internet protocols transparent to the user.

Essential to understanding the World Wide Web is the technique called **hypertext**, which it uses to make links between information that may be located anywhere on the Internet. Hypertext is a very important concept for understanding the impact of emerging technologies on our lives; and we shall discuss its significance in a later chapter (p.70). The term was coined by Ted Nelson in the 1960s. In a hypertext document, any word may become a link to information that may be found elsewhere in the same document or in another document. In an ordinary text, for example, an author may refer to another text, either in parentheses within the text itself or in a footnote. To read this second text, to which the footnote refers, I would need to find it and read it as another document. That might take some time. If it is not on my bookshelf, I might check in a local bookstore or library. If the work is out of print and is not in the local library, it may take days or weeks to get the text through Interlibrary Loan.

In the case of an ordinary reference, then, the first text *points to* the second, but is not *linked to* it. In a hypertext, by contrast, the reader can jump at once from the first text to the second and call up immediately any other information referred to in the hypertext.

The computer makes hypertext possible. While it is difficult to imagine how one might "jump" instantly from a page in a printed book to another document, it is easy to imagine on a computer. The "help" function in many computer programmes which run on a Macintosh or under Windows uses a kind of hypertext that makes it possible to move from one topic to a related one simply by "clicking" on a word or phrase.

Imagine that this book were a hypertext. You would be able to touch or "click" on the underlined word "hypertext" in the previous sentence. At once, you would be presented with another text, which might list a number of documents about hypertext, with the title of each underlined. These would be **links**, which you could select in order to call up the actual text of the document listed in this select bibliography. If you go on to imagine that each of these texts contains links to other documents, you begin to see how hypertext extends itself into a whole web of information.

A web-like structure by its very nature offers many options for how one will engage information. The way people actually use hypertext — following link after link, jumping from one document to another without necessarily reading any from beginning to end — has suggested the two verbs most commonly used to describe the activity of using the World Wide Web: "browse" and "surf".

Once you have connected to the Internet, you can use your Web browser to view any World Wide Web page you like. Your browser may connect you automatically to a "starting" page (Netscape Navigator connects you to Netscape's home page, Internet Explorer to Microsoft's), but you can change your starting page to whatever you like or elect to have no standard starting page.

To get to another page, you must either follow a link from your starting page or enter the **URL** ("Universal Resource Locator") for the page you wish to see. A URL may be though of as simply a Web address. For example, the URL of my own Web page is "http://www.inter-change.ubc.ca/dml/". The first part indicates that what you will find at this address is a Web page (a Web browser is capable of accessing more than just Web pages). The first part of the address — "http://" — stands for "Hypertext Transfer Protocol", the protocol or ritual used by computers to exchange information in the form of Web pages. The second part — "www.interchange.ubc.ca" — tells your Internet provider where my page will be found on the internet: it is the address of the service "Interchange" on the computers of the University of British Columbia (ubc) in Canada (ca). The third part of the address consists of my initials (dml), which is how I am identified on the University of British Columbia computer. It tells the University of British Columbia computer where to look for my Web page.

Of the several ways of finding information on the World Wide Web, browsing is probably the most fun but also the least efficient. One starts anywhere on the Web and looks for what one wants by following promising links. If you are looking for something general, you will undoubtedly find something of interest, whereas if you are looking for something specific, it may take a long time to locate exactly what you need. For example, through a simple following of links from "religion" or "Eastern thought and culture", it would not take long to find *something* on Buddhism. But if you need specific information about the Kyoto school of Buddhist thought, for example, simply following links is a rather haphazard or random way.

A second, more direct method of using the Web involves using a Web index. One of the most popular indexes is called Yahoo (at the URL "http://www.yahoo.com"). In using Yahoo, you start with a list of some very broad categories — arts and humanities, business, computing, recreation, and the like. Under "religion" (found under the general heading "society and culture") you can select "Buddhism" and from there go on to check out the listings that seem most promising for finding references to the "Kyoto school". While this method is much more efficient than simple browsing, it will not find the information you are looking for if it is hidden in an unlikely place.

The third method is the most promising — although given the present state-of-the art, it does not always live up to its promise. This method involves the use of a "search engine". Search engines are services that read millions of Web sites and generate indexes of the words found there. These are maintained and regularly updated in large databases. At the time of writing, one of the best search engines is Alta Vista (at the URL "http://www.altavista.digital.com"). When you reach the main page of Alta Vista you are invited to enter the word or words for which you are searching — "Kyoto school", for example. In a few seconds, Alta Vista will provide you with a list of sites, the most promising of which are at the top of the list.

The World Wide Web, in effect, allows us to treat all of the resources on the hundreds of thousands of computers connected to the Internet as a gigantic, global hypertext. The treasury of information to which one can have access through the Web is virtually infinite. As the Web grows, and as more sophisticated ways for locating information are developed, it has the promise of putting the resources of a global library at the command of any personal computer.

Much of the hype surrounding the World Wide Web today has to do with what is often called "multimedia". Generally, when one hears of a "hot site" on the Web, what makes it "hot" is not the quality of information it carries but its innovative use of graphic and multimedia techniques. "Hypertext" allows traditional text, graphics, audio and video signals to be integrated on a single Web "page". Thus, it is possible to have a telephone conversation, hear a musical number or see a television clip over the Web.

However, before getting carried away with the possibilities, we need to be aware of the limits of what is practical today. The fact is that the techniques for sending audio and video signals over the Internet are in their infancy. Most modems today cannot meet the demands of sophisticated audio and video transmissions. Furthermore, there is a limit to how much information the Internet facilities can handle at any moment; and at peak times the Internet slows down and each user has to wait for his or her turn. The result, especially annoying in multimedia transmissions, is a very jerky, if not unacceptably discontinuous presentation. A Mozart symphony or a rock band performance loses its effect if each musical phrase is randomly interrupted for several seconds as the Internet gives other people their turn.

The information superhighway

The term "information superhighway" was not coined to describe the Internet. Much of the early discussion of the information superhighway saw the Internet as an *example* of what an information superhighway might be like, but the expression tended to stick and many people today use the terms as synonyms and think of the Internet as the information superhighway.

The Internet was developed to connect computers. It started as a tool for military research and involved government, military, university and industrial users. From that nucleus it has grown to become a far-flung network connecting clients of all types from multinational corporations to hobbyists. But it is still a network of computers. The information superhighway refers to something more: it is the dream of a network that carries information of all types, the Internet, the telephone system and cable systems for television and radio all integrated in one network.

As far as the information superhighway is concerned, we are not quite there yet. We have the basic technologies. All communication is becoming digital. As it does, the possibility of common digital networks becomes possible. From the point of view of the transmission of information, every digital signal looks the same. But even where the technology exists, the implementation of those technologies may be complicated by economic and political interests. Can governments sanction a movement of information that pays no attention to national boundaries? Can telephone companies and cable companies agree to a technology which implies that one (telephone or cable) will absorb the other? Who will control the superhighway? Who will pay for it? Whose interests will it serve?

The Internet is what we have now as a model for a global information network. It represents a transition from the forms of communication that dominated the past to the forms of communication that are yet to come. But even if it is destined to pass away, it is a significant harbinger of our future. It represents a world that we need to come to know.

3. The Online Church
A Brief History

The mainframe mentality:
the church and number-crunching

The first computers, which appeared in the 1940s and 1950s, were very large and consisted of masses of vacuum tubes linked together by miles of wire. Because they consumed a great deal of energy and generated considerable heat, they occupied special rooms. Not surprisingly, they were very expensive; and at the outset they were solely the property of governments. The first computer applications had to do with sophisticated calculations related to the needs of the combatants in the second world war.

After the war, and especially when transistors began to replace the larger and more expensive vacuum tubes in the 1950s, computers began to be acquired by large businesses and universities. These computers, produced by firms like Univac and IBM, were still large and very expensive and still required special rooms. They were used as "number crunchers", for applications requiring the processing of large numbers of often repetitive calculations. They might be used, for example, for generating the monthly bills of a large corporation — like a telephone company — from the information on file about each individual account.

Throughout the 1950s and 1960s, as computers became progressively smaller and less expensive, more and more businesses and organizations acquired them to assist with administrative tasks such as financial management and record-keeping. It was during this period that many denominations began to use computers for these purposes in their central administrative offices.

The paradox of computer development over the first fifty or so years of its existence has been that as computers became smaller and cheaper, their powers have increased: they have become faster and capable of handling more information. The development of minicomputers in the 1970s meant that comparatively small and affordable computers became available to many organizations, not only in their central offices but in regional offices as well. The development of specialized computers called "word-processors" during the 1970s further placed computers (although disguised by a different name) in the offices even of comparatively small organizations of all types, including churches.

Ministry and "ad-ministry"

During the late 1970s, even smaller and cheaper computers came onto the market. Seen at first primarily as hobbyist machines, these computers had much of the speed and capacity that would have been available only in large mainframe computers a decade earlier. With the appearance of the IBM PC in 1980, these small personal computers, which fit easily on an office desk, were able to make the transition in the popular mind from hobbyists' toys to serious business machines; and as desktop computers gained acceptance as business machines, they began to appear in church offices, even in local congregations.

At the same time, the use of desktop computers had been growing among ministers, priests and active laypeople in the church. The stage was thus set for a period in which the churches sought to find their way between two quite different views of computers. The churches had entered the computer world through the mainframe mentality. In other words, they had seen the computer as something designed for the church's "ad-ministry", a business machine for dealing with centralized management functions. The clergy who first placed computers on their desks were informed by another notion of computers. This "hobbyist" view of them drew on a tradition that goes back to the early "hackers", those enthusiasts who from the early 1960s on had managed to gain access to computers, usually in universities, and saw them as something to be played with. As Steven Levy observes in his study of computer culture, hackers became involved with computers to test their limits, to see what they could do. Father Hal Stockert, a Byzantine-rite Catholic priest from upstate New York who was one of the earliest small computer users in the church, made this comment (in personal correspondence with the author):

> The "hackers" weren't interested in the appearances of power or the trappings. They weren't interested (though some now are) in the hierarchical advancement they might bring. They subliminally understood the differences and distinctions between "power" on the one hand and "authority" on the other... The "hackers", whether they knew it or not, were after *real* power, the ability to create change elsewhere — whether there was authority for it or not.

The ministers and active laity who became involved with computers in the early 1980s inherited something of this attitude. They began to explore computers as tools for ministry. Thus John Easton, a layperson and computer enthusiast in Toronto, designed computer games and other software for use in Christian education, which he installed on computers that were placed in the Sunday school of his congregation. Father Stockert designed software — still in use — which allowed churches to track member contributions, attendance and pastoral visitations. David Martyn, a pastor in Terrace, a small community in the interior of British Columbia, designed a programme which assisted him in choosing hymns. I designed a programme for comparing how different theologians used the Bible in their theological writings. These programmes were designed, not so much because they met a clearly defined need or improved the way traditional tasks could be done, but more in order to see what could be done, to explore the possibilities of small computers for ministry.

The tension between the use of the computer in adminstry and in ministry pervaded discussions of relevance of computer technology in the church during the 1980s. Congregations could often see the sense in putting a computer on the secretary's desk but not in installing one in the minister's study. Theological schools provided computers for their stenographic pool but not for their professors. Denominational offices often had difficulty in understanding why programme staff might need a computer. So while the administrative use of computers expanded in church offices, it was the enthusiasts who spurred the non-administrative, programme-oriented use of computers in the church.

Often, the interest in computers as a tool for ministry focused on the ability of computers to communicate. Computers had long been used for communication. Building on teletype technology, computer signals were sent like teletype messages over telephone lines. Lew Wilkins describes an early use — in 1974 — of computers to communicate for ecclesiastical purposes:

> I was serving on a long-range planning committee of a newly-formed presbytery. We had gathered data from every congregation and, in one of those arduous processes, cast it in the form of twelve goal statements that the presbytery as a body was to rank in priority order. How to do that ranking in a decision-making body designed to make simple, yes-or-no decisions was the nut we had to crack.
>
> By chance, I was talking about our problem with a layman who happened to work for GE Timeshare computer services. Together we designed a simple forced-choice instrument for each presbyter to complete, to produce a personal ranking. My GE friend wrote a little programme for the GE mainframe in Cleveland, Ohio, to take 150 individual rankings of the twelve items and compile them into the presbytery's ranking.
>
> On the night of the presbytery meeting, we had the ministers and elders fill out their rating forms. Then we sat for about three hours in front of one of those big old teletype terminals, keypunching the data into a paper strip that curled and curled onto the floor.
>
> The magic moment came at about one o'clock in the morning, when we finally dialled the Cleveland phone number from our little church office in New Orleans, Louisiana, put the handset in the acoustical cradle on the terminal, heard modems make their noises for the first time, and fed the paper tape through the machine.
>
> About 20 seconds after the tape cleared the machine, it began to print out our twelve goal statements — ranked in priority order and with the tally of ranking scores by each one. From New Orleans, we made something happen in Cleveland, and the computer in Cleveland told us what we had done. It was about as simple an information transaction as I can imagine, but

enough to convince me that there was something here worth knowing about.

In the late 1960s a network was created so that scientists involved in defence research in the United States could communicate quickly and securely. This network of universities and defence establishments was the precursor to what is known today as the Internet. At the same time, the needs of businesses, particularly international corporations, to share data between the computers of their various branches, spurred the growth of commercial "packet switching networks". These networks made it possible to send data across continents and around the world in a way that was more efficient than by using long distance telephone calls. Some services — MCI Mail and Dialcom are among the best-known — were created to allow electronic mail to be sent between people in different organizations in widely separated places. Many of these were established to serve organizations rather than individuals; and some churches, looking to use electronic mail to communicate between their offices, established accounts with them. Still, access to electronic mail tended to be limited to administrative and programme officers and not to extend to ministers of local congregations and lay volunteers.

The growth of the "enthusiast" community of computer users, however, led to other developments. Some companies who found themselves with their expensive mainframes sitting unused outside of office hours hit on the idea of allowing hobbyists access to their unused computer power during evening and early morning hours. As the community of computer enthusiasts grew, some of these services expanded until consumer online access became their primary reason for existence. The giant online service Compuserve began in this way.

Among the enthusiasts who were early users of these online services were church people looking for ways to use this new means of communication to express their religious interests. On Compuserve, for example, a lively religious forum was established under the direction of Donald McKim, then a theology professor in the Presbyterian seminary in Dubuque, Iowa. Since then, religious discussion of one kind or another has become a feature of almost every major online service.

Father Stockert was an early presence on many early online services in the United States. He used one of the first BBS, run by Ward Christensen in Chicago, from the time it started in February 1978; and, invited by Jack Taub, the founder of one of the early commercial online services, to use his new service The Source, Stockert became a pioneer user there.

Another priest and theological professor, Patrick Gaffney, used the user-publishing facility to publish a Christology text on The Source, possibly the first book to be written, edited and published online. Gaffney used the text as the basis of an online "course" which became a means by which he and Stockert exercised a ministry among online Catholics, both active and disaffected.

Another early freelance online ministry was that of Bob Cramer, a Baptist (now a member of the United Church of Christ) from northern California. As a young man, Cramer had worked in the communications offices of both denominational and ecumenical organizations. By the 1980s he had established his own consulting business and acted as a gadfly to the denominational and ecumenical communications offices he had once worked for. Using very basic equipment, Cramer set up a religious news service on an online service called Newsnet, a large collection of newsletters, most with a business orientation. Through Cramer's efforts, the United Methodist Church in the United States for a while published its news releases on the same service. Around the same time, the Lutheran Church in America launched an experimental news service on The Source under the direction of Charles Austin, a former religion writer for *The New York Times*, and Kris Lee, who was later instrumental in developing the international Anglican online network Quest.

The emergence of the online church

The Church Computer Users' Network (CCUN) was a US organization of early computer enthusiasts in the church. From its base in the United Methodist Church, it had become by the mid-1980s an ecumenical and national organization. Richard Spady, a United Methodist layperson from Seattle, Washington, was a businessman turned futurist with an enthusiasm for the new media; and he arranged with the University of Washington to provide some basic online services for CCUN.

The United Methodists were not the only denomination looking with interest at the online world. The growing number of enthusiasts with access to a computer and modem led to some early experiments in denominational networking in the mid-1980s. Among evangelicals, the development of local bulletin board systems was popular. A BBS could be installed on almost any desktop computer and connected to a telephone line; and such a system, typically operated by an individual, could function as a kind of "storefront" ministry, providing not only a discussion forum for local evangelicals, but also an outreach to non-Christians who might happen to call. Among so-called mainline denominations on the other hand, interest focused on systems which would be available nationally or even internationally. Several developments were preparing the way for the emergence of ecumenical networking. In June 1984, the ecumenical agency for the support of denominational mission units in North America, the Joint Strategy and Action Committee (JSAC), sponsored a conference in Atlanta to explore computer use in the church. It brought together not only the more traditional mainframe computer users from denominational head offices but also people primarily interested in the potential of personal computers for use in the church. Out of this meeting, the Computer Applications for Ministry Network (CAMNET) was formed. One of the directions that CAMNET recognized as needing development was online computer networking.

Independently, about a month later, Jim Franklin, the religion editor for the Boston *Globe*, entered into discussion with Participate, Inc. concerning the potential of their software — which was used for electronic discussion groups on The Source — for religious groups. As a result, an online meeting called Religious Associates was opened on The Source. It brought together the various people who were to be instrumental in the emergence of ecumenical networking during the next few years. In addition to Franklin, the group included Austin, Cramer, Fathers Gaffney and Stockert, Jim Coolie (a Presbyterian from Texas and longtime participant in Participate discussions), Ian MacDonald, Gordon Laird and myself (all of the United Church of Canada), Curt Ackley (United Church of Christ), Nelson Murphy (Reformed Church in America) and Susan Peek (United Methodist Church). Peek, Murphy and I had also participated in the JSAC Atlanta conference.

Over the ten months from November 1984, three separate denominational initiatives were launched. The United Church of Christ, under the direction of Eugene Schneider, conducted an experiment in denominational networking on Compuserve. This was followed by a similar experiment, again on Compuserve, conducted by the Presbyterian Church (USA). And the United Church of Canada inaugurated its own denominational network, UCHUG ("United Church Users' Group"). The name reflects its "enthusiast" orientation, "Users' Group" being a common term to designate organizations of computer hobbyists. Despite efforts to find a more inclusive sounding acronym the name has persisted. The contacts made in Religious Associates proved to be a catalyst moving the denominational initiatives in an ecumenical direction. Cramer was involved in one way or another with all three projects; Ackley participated in both the United Church of Christ and Presbyterian experiments.

The United Church of Canada network, after six months on the Canadian electronic mail service Envoy 100, moved to the small American service Unison, which used the Participate software, with its ability to branch discussions simply and by any member, thus making it one of the best systems to promote the kind of networking desired by the church groups. Stockert, who was usually one step ahead of the others in exploring new online systems, had already established a small Catholic network, Fishnet, on the Unison system.

Meanwhile, the Presbyterian experiment on Compuserve was creating considerable enthusiasm. Collie, Wilkins and Huston Hodges created an online magazine, *Monday Night Connection*. Jack Sharp started the lectionary discussion group to which we referred earlier. He recalls the initial experience:

> Each week I prepared some exegetical materials and posted them on Sermonshop. At first there were no more than 10-15 persons using the materials, but we soon had a vibrant discussion group. I can recall the notes of gratitude from a minister in an isolated part of Iowa. It was during the times when farmers were losing their land through repossession. The minister had conducted funerals of several suicides and had many despondent members in his congregation. Over the next year he relied upon Sermonshop for emotional and theological assistance. Several presbyteries made weekly mimeographed copies of the materials and distributed it to their ministers. There was a growing sense that a large "support group" was being formed through the technology.

As the Presbyterian experiment on Compuserve approached its conclusion, the denominational sponsors gave no inkling of what might happen next. The enthusiasts, however, having had a taste of what the medium might offer, looked around for a new home. After considering a number of options, this group of Presbyterian "refugees" established an unofficial Presbyterian network, Presbynet, on Unison in the fall of 1985. In the six months that followed, the Presbyterians, the United Church of Canada group and the United Church of Christ (represented primarily by Ackley, Schneider and Donel McLelland) went through a sometimes rocky process of building an informal ecumenical online community.

A critical period came in early 1986. The national communications office of the Presbyterian Church (USA) — on the basis of the Compuserve experiment and after investigating a variety of online services including Unison — announced that the permanent electronic home for the Presbyterian network would be NETI, a new service funded by venture capital, which was developing its own conferencing software called E-Forum. Although the Presbyterian "refugees" on Unison reacted unhappily, a training event was scheduled for late February where the most active users of the Compuserve experiment (almost all of whom were among the Unison "refugees") were introduced to the new system.

At issue were both technology and ideology. The NETI system had been designed from a managerial perspective. It allowed multiple discussions, but each separate "meeting" could be opened only by a system administrator. The Participate system, as noted, allowed anyone to start a new meeting on any topic that she or he chose. So, although the Presbyterians Unison "refugees" participated in NETI, their prime commitment remained with the ecumenical group that met on Unison. There were in effect two Presbyterian systems: an unofficial Presbynet on Unison and the official system, quickly dubbed "PresbyNETI".

The PresbyNETI project lasted for several years, but there were a number of problems. First, although NETI had raised significant venture capital, its only product — the E-Forum conferencing software — was not sufficiently developed to bring the operating income needed. NETI went out of business around the same time as the end of the Presbyterian contract. Second, the Presbyterian staff promoting the NETI experiment had not adequately consulted those who would be the users of the new system. The enthusiasts, on whom the denomination were depending to make the system work, were already committed to, and promoting, the Participate software. NETI's less flexible E-Forum software, according to Lew Wilkins, was "unworkable":

> It was at least as complex as Parti to learn, and far less transparent to use. E-mail and rudimentary conferencing were in different systems. Moving from one place to another in the

system often was a long journey. Above all, it was always extremely slow. The information management technology in E-Forum called attention to itself and distracted the user from the information that was being managed.

A third factor in the failure of PresbyNETI was that other denominations and "ecumenical partners" had not been adequately consulted. Only the Lutherans accepted the invitation to join the Presbyterians on the new system; other denominations and the National Council of Churches were looking with growing interest at the developing ecumenical network on Unison.

While this crisis was brewing, the Unison networks had been learning much about the ecumenical power of the new method of communication. This was most vividly illustrated in January 1986, when the space shuttle *Challenger* was destroyed shortly after takeoff. The world watched as the image of an explosion in the blue sky over Florida was replayed and replayed and replayed.

It was a moment that stunned the world; and the owners of Unison approached the church groups to ask if they could organize something online. The result was "Memorial Service", an online liturgy planned in a single day by Ackley, Collie, Laird and Michael Henderson, a Methodist in South Carolina. It presented a memorial liturgy with prayers, scripture, meditation and a section in which readers could add their own prayers. Finally, in a "Coffee Hour" (a meeting designed for general discussion) those who had followed the online liturgy could share their own feelings about the tragedy. "Memorial Service" demonstrated the power of the computer medium to unite a community in a time of crisis beyond the limits of geography or denomination.

The first conference (CAMCON) sponsored by CAM-NET, the organization that had been formed at the Atlanta meeting, was held in Los Angeles immediately following the Presbyterian NETI training event. For the first time, most of the leading participants in the Unison network met face-to-face. Most of the CAMCON attendees had given little thought to the computer as a means of communication; and the energy of the Unison group gave them a visibility far beyond their numbers, helping to give the group a clear sense of its own identity.

By summer 1986, however, it became clear to the leadership of the church networks that Unison was in serious financial difficulty. If Unison's creditors were to "pull the plug" without warning, they could be left electronically homeless. To deal with the crisis, the United Church of Canada group supplied accounts on the Canadian e-mail system Envoy 100, where the network leaders could discuss the situation and possible alternatives confidentially. Through these discussions, the group explicitly recognized that they represented a de facto ecumenical network. They had evolved a sense of identity as a community that existed independently of whatever electronic service they chose for their electronic communication. At this time, the group began to refer to this community as "Ecunet".

The pressing question was where Ecunet would have its electronic home. The larger online services like Compuserve and The Source seemed too expensive. One of the group arranged complimentary accounts on a San Francisco-based service, The Web, to be explored as a possible home. Another contacted Sherwin Levinson, who was running a new service called NWI.

Levinson had been associated with earlier ventures in church-related computing. He had been a consultant to the Presbyterian Church in their exploration of the new media, and had attended the Los Angeles CAMCON as a workshop leader in computer communications. NWI used the same Participate software that the Ecunet group had used on Unison. Levinson made an offer which the group accepted; and in November 1986 it was announced that Ecunet would have its new home on NWI.

From November 1986 to May 1990, Ecunet developed, using the services of NWI, into the official online arm of North American churches. A workshop sponsored by the National Council of Churches in September 1986 gave its tacit blessing to the Ecunet concept. Ecunet incorporated in the spring of 1987 with a number of denominational representatives on its board. When its contract with NETI expired, the communications unit of the Presbyterian Church (USA) recognized the Presbyterian presence on NWI as its official network. The United Methodist Church transferred its activities from the University of Washington computer to NWI. An Ecunet BBS network, using the facilities of Fidonet, was coordinated by Jack Sharp in Baltimore.

In May 1990, for reasons beyond the control of its management, NWI failed. Response was immediate. The Presbyterian Church (USA) provided computers at its Louisville headquarters; Levinson and former NWI president Phil Moore formed the Online Service Company to supply technical and administrative services; and within days, Ecunet — now hosted by Presbynet — was up and running again.

Since 1990, Ecunet and its member networks have experienced continued growth. From the handful of enthusiasts that had inhabited Unison in 1985, Ecunet has expanded to a network of well over 5000 people. Through the initiative of the worldwide Anglican network Quest, and through the work of David Pozzi-Johnson of the World Council of Churches, Ecunet has been extending its constituency. Today Ecunet may be reached through any Internet provider anywhere in the world; and many of its "meetings" are available to Internet users through mailing lists. A support group for women, both ordained and lay, called "Women in Ministry Online", originating as an Ecunet meeting, is distributed by Internet mailing list to women in Europe, North America and Australia.

4. The Digital Word
Gospel and Information

In one way or another, the church has always been in the communication business. At different times and in different traditions, the interpretation of exactly what the church is in the business of communicating might vary. To some, the church is in the business of communicating truth, pure doctrine. Others would prefer to emphasize the work of the church as an agent of the outpouring of God's grace through the sacraments. Still others would speak of the church's prime responsibility as that of preaching the gospel, the word of God.

The centrality of the word for the church, its responsibility for communication, pervades the church's life, history and thought. The world is created through God's Word. Jesus Christ is the Word made flesh. The sacraments are the visible words of God. Proclamation of the Word of God is entrusted by God to the church.

What is the relationship of the word which God speaks and to which the church bears witness on the one hand, and what the contemporary world calls information on the other? This is not a simple question to answer. There are important differences between the Word, that which is communicated in the gospel, and information as it is understood in a digital world. At the same time, there are important continuities between gospel and information. But let us start with the differences.

Understanding information

Recall the lowly bit. As we have seen, computers process bits. These bits can be in one of two states: "on" or "off", "1" or "0". In a digital world, "information" is anything that can be reduced to a "stream" of bits. A bit, then, is an atom of information, out of which more complex forms of information can be constructed. All information is ultimately reducible to bits.

If this is so, some important consequences follow. The bit has two qualities which have consequences for how we understand information. First, as a unit of information, it is completely *abstract*. As we have already seen, a bit can represent anything. Second, the bit is *unambiguous*. It is either in one state or another. There are no uncertainties in digitized information. Every unit in the digital stream is either "on" or "off". There is no middle ground.

From a theological perspective, these two elements of the digital model of information leave us with some suspicion. The "Word", regardless of how we explain it theologically, is not abstract. Any Christian understanding of word draws its meaning from the "Word made flesh". The Word of the Christian gospel is an incarnate word. When God speaks, the communication takes a concrete human form. Second, when the Word is spoken, we human beings who "hear" the "Word" are confronted with mystery. In the revelation of God, mystery is not dissolved. As Rudolf Otto showed in his classic study *The Idea of the Holy*, the God who is encountered in revelation is and remains the *mysterium tremendum*.

The digital model of information has no room for mystery. The world it constructs is simply the sum of the bits. Information in this sense is "flat". It has no depth. Everything is on the surface. There is nothing but bits — the 1s and the 0s that make up the digital universe. Digital information makes no distinction between appearance and reality, true and false, meaningful and meaningless. There is just information — data.

We cannot help speaking paradoxically here. Information is not "true". It is not "false" either. While it may seem strange to speak of information as not "true", the point is a simple one. Those things we would designate as true or false fill only a small corner of the information universe. Even if information conveys something false, it is still "information". But most types of information have little to do with truth or falsity at all.

I have in front of me a compact disk. It is filled with information: streams of bits. The label on it tells me that the information contained on the disk represents Beethoven's Symphony Number 9, Opus 125. What this means is that if I interpret the information on the disk in a certain way — by playing it through an appropriately equipped stereo system

— the information will be translated into sounds which most people with a modicum of musical knowledge would recognize as Beethoven's Ninth Symphony.

In this example — and we might have substituted any one of a whole range of other ways in which we use digital information — questions of truth or falsity never arise. We can see this more clearly by considering how something could have "gone wrong" in this example.

First case: When I play the disk, I hear a very poor quality reproduction of the work. The high or low tones (or both) seem to be missing. The sound at best can be described as "tinny". In this case we would say that the sound quality is "degraded", that it is a "poor reproduction" of the original performance. But we would not say that the information is "false".

Second case: When I play the disk, I hear nothing but noise — static — from the speakers. Now there are a number of reasons this might happen. The fault might be in my stereo system. It might be with the disk itself. To describe this situation we would probably say that either the disk or the stereo system is "defective". We would go about trying to discover which of the two was at fault. But we would not say that the information on the disk was "false".

Third case: When I listen to the disk, what I hear is not Beethoven's Ninth Symphony but the Grand March from Verdi's *Aida*. In this case we might use the term "false", but not of the digital information on the disk itself. We should say that the disk was "mislabelled", that if anything was "false" it was the title that had been printed on the disk. It would not occur to us to say that the data — that which gets interpreted by the stereo system as sound — is either "true" or "false".

Now I have before me another disk. It is a CD-ROM labelled *Myst*. I know that if I attempt to play it through a stereo system the result will not be pleasant. Like the Beethoven disk, this disk also contains information — lots of it. But the information on this disk is not meant to be interpreted solely as sound. It is a computer programme which includes both graphics and sound. If it is run on a certain type of computer (in the case of this particular disk, a computer which is using Windows 95), then it will do what it is supposed to do. What it is supposed to do can be described this way: *Myst* is a game which creates five interconnected worlds for the player to explore and "figure out". It is an exploration in fantasy.

We shall not look here at the various ways things could "go wrong" with *Myst*, except to say that analogous misadventures to those we imagined with the digital recording of Beethoven could happen with a CD-ROM. What we need to notice is how this example has removed us one more step from any notion of "truth" and "falsity".

In the case of the Beethoven symphony, we were still making our judgments within a framework of referential logic. In other words, we believe that there is something "out there in the real world" that we could label "Beethoven's Ninth Symphony". For our purposes here we can pass over the question of just what is meant by saying that the symphony is "out there"; the point is that we expect that what is on the disk will correspond, in some important sense, to something that is not on the disk but exists or existed elsewhere. To make this claim as conservatively as possible, we can say that what is on this disk "corresponds to" a certain performance of the symphony by the Berlin Philharmonic Orchestra under the direction of the late Herbert von Karajan. In this sense, then, we assume a relationship between the information on the disk and something in the "real world". This relationship — which we have characterized as one of correspondence — is one that many (though not all) philosophers would acknowledge as the relationship we call "truth".

In the case of *Myst*, even this relationship does not hold. *Myst* does not "represent" anything "out there". Instead it draws the reader into a world (or, better, "worlds") that "exist" nowhere but in "cyberspace" itself. It makes little sense to think of *Myst* as being "true" or "false".

Of course, one might object that there is nothing surprising or significant about this example. In this respect *Myst* resembles any work of fiction. A good work of fiction creates a world. It does not "represent" anything "out there". Or we could think of other examples. Does poetry "represent" anything? Sometimes it does. Sometimes it does not.

The objection can be granted. Indeed it makes precisely the point that we need to make here. Fiction, poetry and the like are not usually evaluated as "true" or "false", but both poetry and fiction would be included in what we mean by "information".

Seen through the lens of digital technology, information does not have to be true or false; more paradoxically, it does not even have to be meaningful. Bare data, as we have observed, are nothing more than streams of bits. One stream of bits looks much like another. As we represent a stream of bits in print, they look like random sequences of 1s and 0s. Can we speak of the "meaning" of something like "0010111001100111111010011"? This sequence contains quite definite information. Change the order of the 1s and 0s and it would represent different information. The "information" contained in our sequence consists precisely in the order and the number of the bits.

But what does it mean? The "meaning" of the sequence depends on how we choose to interpret it. The bits could represent anything — letters, numbers, points of light, musical frequencies — and the "meaning" of this scrap of information will differ according to what we take the bits to represent. Whether it is a word, a picture, a sound, a statistic all depends on our interpretation. We cannot read the meaning from the data itself.

Can information be Christian?

"Information" as understood in information technology may seem a poor vehicle for that communication which is at the heart of Christian faith. Indeed, we may find them so incommensurable that we are inclined to say that the contemporary concept of information has no relevance to the communication of the Christian gospel. Bare data, which is what the contemporary concept of information comes to, might seem so degraded and trivial from a Christian point of view as to be of no interest to Christian communicators. Data do not transform the human heart. Faith is not a matter of having reliable statistics. Hope is not a matter of the projection of trends into the future. The word of God cannot be reduced to bits.

However, we cannot escape the problem that simply. Computers have made their way into our offices and our studies. We use computers for electronic mail. Willingly or unwillingly, we are being drawn into an era where "to exist" is seen more and more in terms of having a fax number, an e-mail address and a Web page. A few of us may have the luxury of not having to use a computer and so remaining untouched by the logic of the digital word. Yet the fact remains that the computer is rapidly becoming a necessity in any enterprise — including the church — that deals with words, ideas, beliefs and the like. If it is true that more than a few of my colleagues in the church and in academia, especially those over 50, still use a typewriter and will probably never use a word-processor, it is also true that almost all the student essays I am asked to read have been prepared on a computer. On the personal level we may be able to resist the incursion of the computer into our lives, but on the cultural level we are living through a shift that will have as powerful a transformative effect as the introduction of printing in the 15th and 16th centuries.

Information understood as a stream of binary digits, as "data", seems then to be a poor model for the kind of communication which is at the heart of the gospel. But we must set this observation in the context of another: that in the past few centuries, we have allowed our thinking to be dominated by a model of communication that fits closely with the kind of communication which is "at home" on the printed page — the model of truth as knowledge, the representation of objective reality.

Print externalizes truth. It creates a kind of communication that is "out there", reducing what is communicated to something completely visual. What we read is apprehended through our eyes in a form that is uniform, repeatable and "objective". Print constructs reality by representing it as what the philosopher Ludwig Wittgenstein called a "totality of facts".

Print is the medium *par excellence* of what philosophers and cultural critics call "modernity". The culture of print is oriented to the discovery of facts, to the "truth" of the external universe, which can be validated by the kind of rational argument that is most at home on the printed page. The model of communication based on the printed word focuses attention on how our language can be said accurately to represent the world "out there". Religious apologists in this culture have thus tended to represent what is at the heart of their traditions as essentially a matter of describing what is ultimately true about the universe. The difference between religious traditions is interpreted as a question of which religion most accurately describes the ultimate nature of reality.

The history of Western Christianity during the last 500 years has involved a constant struggle with the concept of communication fostered by the print medium. This model of truth as objective fact has led many to interpret the communication of the gospel as a matter of defending and propagating "true" doctrine. Yet there have always been some who have reacted strongly against any attempt to reduce the Christian gospel to objective fact.

In the 17th century, René Descartes attempted to construct a new model of knowledge which would allow thinkers to construct a true and certain view of reality. In his philosophical vision, God became a kind of ultimate fact. The knowledge of God — that is the certainty of God's existence and perfection — became the foundation for a sure grasp of objective reality. Descartes's philosophical achievement, however, was called into question by his French contemporary Blaise Pascal, who denounced the "God of the philosophers" in the name of the "God of Abraham, Isaac and Jacob", the living God of Christian faith. For Pascal,

Christian faith was not a matter of objective theory, but of a "wager", the risk of faith.

Pascal's objection to formulating Christian faith on the basis of the modern notion of objective truth has been repeatedly echoed through the succeeding centuries. The emphasis placed on the truth of confessional doctrines during the period of "Protestant scholasticism" in the 16th and 17th centuries produced a reaction in the 17th and 18th centuries in the form of the pietist movements, which insisted that Christian faith was a matter of the "heart" rather than of the "head". Christianity, for the pietistic movements and their descendants, has to do not with an intellectual understanding of doctrine but with personal experience. One becomes a Christian, not through intellectual assent to certain truths about God, but through conversion. Justification and sanctification are essentially a transformation of the heart, not a mere change of opinion.

The reaction of Søren Kierkegaard to the Hegelian philosophy which dominated the 19th-century Danish Lutheran church offers another example of how problematical the modern concept of knowledge has been for the interpretation of the Christian gospel. Using the pseudonym Johannes Climacus, Kierkegaard launched a devastating attack on the concept of "objectivity" in Christian theology, arguing that it distracts the individual from what is at the heart of the gospel, namely the infinite concern about one's eternal happiness. In his time, Climacus claimed, theologians had become so objective that they no longer cared about their eternal happiness. For the Christian, Climacus argued, "subjectivity is truth". In short, what is decisive for Christian faith is our relationship *to* God, not our beliefs *about* God.

What these examples suggest is that the concept of information in which everything is reduced to streams of binary digits is no more problematic for a Christian understanding of communication than the modern model of knowledge as objective fact has been in recent centuries. The problem is not so much whether contemporary models of communication measure up to the communication at the heart of the gospel. Every culturally defined model of communication will exhibit some tension with the needs of Christian faith. The problem is more the classical problem of "Christ and culture", how the Word "takes flesh" in the forms available in the culture in which we live.

Christians have always understood their faith in the light of the categories of their own time. When, for example, truth was understood in terms of wisdom and philosophy was understood as the search for wisdom, Christians often represented the gospel as a divine wisdom, a philosophy which was superior to merely human philosophies because its author was God. When, under the impact of print, truth became a matter of knowledge, of objective fact, Christians moved in the direction of representing the gospel as a set of divinely revealed "facts" which could be discovered in scripture and tradition. As the cultural paradigms shift, the way we articulate the gospel shifts. This is not a matter of syncretism or of being "trendy". It is an aspect of being human. We understand our faith in whatever categories carry credibility in the culture that forms us. Those of us who have been formed by a print culture may well wish to resist the impact of the digitalization of reality. But we do that at the risk of irrelevance. The categories that have been credible in print culture may carry little credibility in the world of our children. Our culture, at the end of the 20th century, is rapidly being transformed into a digital culture. Whatever fears we may have about the consequences of reducing everything to bits, it is important that we understand and be able to relate to this technological revolution that has come upon us.

It has often been observed that we live today in an information age. "Information", it is claimed, is the most important commodity in our economic life today. Much has indeed been reduced to information. Most important in terms of its effect on our day-to-day existence has been the reduction of money to information. Vast quantities of wealth can now be transferred instantly to almost anywhere in the globe. What is actually communicated are bits, but since those bits constitute real wealth, the communication of this information is anything but trivial.

Some benefits of digital words

The digitizing of information is happening because there are significant benefits to be drawn from digital technology. These benefits accrue not only to large multinational corporations, but also to anyone who makes use of these technologies.

Digital technology is able to transcend some of the limitations of earlier technologies. Consider again our compact disk of Beethoven's Ninth Symphony. With this technology, digital signals are burned onto a small disk that can be played in a machine designed to translate those signals into sound. The compact disk replaced two earlier non-digital recording technologies: the vinyl record and the magnetic tape, both of which relied on analogue technologies. That is, they reproduced sound waves by physically storing on the recording medium a wave-form analogous to sound. This sound was then reproduced when the needle of the record player vibrated as it passed through the physical grooves on the vinyl surface of the record, or when the magnetic signals on the tape caused electromagnetic waves to be translated into sounds by the circuitry of a stereo system. With the technology of the CD, a laser beam reads the digital signals burned into the disk. It is not a wave (which mimics the form of sound) but a stream of binary digits that is translated into sound by the electronic circuitry.

It may seem surprising that the quality of sound produced digitally is superior to that of the earlier analogue technologies of vinyl disks and magnetic tapes. There are two reasons for this. One has less to do with the difference between encoding information in analogue or digital form than with the way digital information is reproduced. With vinyl disks and magnetic tape, the recording was "read" by something that came into physical contact with the medium — a needle for the record, the head of the tape deck for the magnetic tape. Both of these techniques tend to wear down the recording surface, resulting in the eventual degradation of the original recording. A CD is read by a laser beam. Since there is no direct physical contact with the disk, repeated playing of a compact disk does not result in a loss of quality of the recorded sound.

But that is not the whole story. The secret of digital technologies is something called "band-width". If very large quantities of binary data can be processed in very short periods of time, a digital recording can come very close to reproducing the original sound. The greater the capacity of the technology to process data (the band-width), the greater the fidelity to the original one can expect. As we noted earlier in this chapter, digital information is very exact. Unlike analogue technologies, which attempt to be an approximate model of an original, a digital message contains no ambiguity at all. Information is either "there" or it is not "there" in the digital message. If it is not "there", the deficiency can usually be remedied by increased band-width. The virtual simultaneity of the speed at which data is processed enables the essentially "flat" stream of binary digits to create the impression of richness and depth.

Digital dualism

Digital technology often surprises us with what it is able to do. We expect computers, which work by reducing everything to bits, to depersonalize whatever they touch, but our experience often confounds this expectation and their effect is to add richness, variety, even intimacy to human life. This personalizing dimension of computer technology was expressed in a slogan popular in the 1980s: "High tech, high touch".

Let us consider computer communication — e-mail and electronic conferencing. By using the computer, we can communicate with people scattered all over the world. We have seen how computer technology allows a kind of communication which is both instantaneous and asynchronous, freeing us from the constraints of space and time which severely limit other kinds of communication.

The speed and convenience of computer communication do not free us of our suspicions. Granted the efficiency of the medium, is it still not depersonalizing? Real personal relationship, we want to say, depends on physical presence. Genuine human communication is more than a matter of words. Our body language, our touch, the tone of our voices, the expression of our eyes — all these belong to the fullness of human communication and relationship. A form of communication that lacks these dimensions of physical presence can only be a shadow of what true personal communication must be.

Two observations should be made here. The first has to do with what Howard Rheingold has called "virtual community". The speed of computer communication can make a qualitative difference between an electronic exchange and the slower methods of correspondence of the past. Although all the physical dimensions of a face-to-face encounter are absent in electronic mail and conferencing, the instantaneous transmission of electronic messages creates what we may describe as a "virtual presence". I first experienced this in 1984 when I spent the better part of a day exchanging short e-mail messages with a friend who was over 2000 miles away. The effect of the flurry of messages that went back and forth across the continent was that I felt as if I had been talking to someone in the next room. In that conversation my friend and I were virtually present to each other. We discussed, we joked, we argued — in short, we enjoyed each other's presence.

Any medium of communication has the power to form community. In the 1930s and 1940s radio allowed Franklin D. Roosevelt to create a sense of intimate community between the president and the people of the United States through his Fireside Chats. At the same time, Adolf Hitler was using the same medium to forge a community of nation and race in Nazi Germany. Even today, radio talk shows allow groups of people, particularly those who feel alienated and dispossessed in contemporary society, a sense of identity and common interest. Television has a similar power to simulate community, particularly around events of national and international crisis: the assassination of John Kennedy, the explosion of the *Challenger* space mission, the Gulf war and so on.

"Virtual community" is the product of computer communication. Through the communications infrastructure provided by long distance telephone, commercial packet-switching networks, online services like Compuserve or America Online and the Internet, it is possible to be in daily communication, at a relatively modest cost, with people scattered around the world. Unlike the anonymous "communities" created by the mass media, the communities made possible by computer communications tend to be small and intimate.

The global reach of computer communication fosters the formation of affinity groups in a way not possible on a local level. If, for example, I have a passion for the writings of Søren Kierkegaard, I may have difficulty in finding someone in my own community who shares my passion. But online I can join the Internet mailing list or discussion group devoted to Kierkegaard, giving me access to others around the world who share my interest. If I become an active participant in a group like this, I soon have a sense of being part of a very real, if unseen, community.

Ecunet had its origins as just such a community, as we saw in the previous chapter. A relatively small number of enthusiasts from all over North America discovered each other online and quickly became a community who, through their daily contact, developed a vision of ecumenical computer communication into a service that includes many denominations and thousands of members. In consequence, Ecunet today is too big to be considered a single community and is rather a community of communities. As new topics of discussion are opened, small communities form around them. These communities are overlapping, since users tend to join a number of discussions and build a sense of community around the particular meetings in which they happen to be active at a given time. Any particular discussion in which one is active may include some people one has encountered in other discussions. By the same token, online communities are ephemeral. In a face-to-face meeting, one is always aware of who is in attendance.

Our second observation has to do with the complete absence of physical clues in electronic conversation. In this medium, nothing physical is exchanged. A message is transmitted as a stream of bits and, as we have said, there is nothing physical about a bit.

Digital communication has often been described as mind-to-mind communication. This technology seems to fulfill the ideal of freeing the soul from the body which characterized Greek philosophy and was taken over by some streams of Christian theology. Since I do not see my correspondent's body, when someone sends me an e-mail message, I have no physical clues to help the communication: no gestures, facial expressions or tones of voice, not even a piece of paper with my correspondent's handwriting or signature — the minimal physical clues present when I receive a letter by mail.

The removal of the body as a factor in communication is of great concern to some critics, who claim that digital technology removes us from contact with physical reality. This has to do with more than merely the absence of body language and the conclusions we draw from it in digital communication. The point is that in cyberspace we can construct worlds that have no connection with physical reality. The idea of virtual reality typifies the ability of the computer to construct non-physical worlds. By the use of special equipment like goggles, earphones and gloves a computer can simulate an environment quite different from the one our bodies inhabit at a particular time. We can experience multiple worlds, all generated by a computer programme.

Mark Slouka has argued that the digital media thus plunge us into a kind of psychosis. For Slouka the real world is the physical, non-technologically mediated world. Reality is "rocks and trees and skies and seas", the world of nature, untainted by the intrusions of technology. Slouka sees the battle lines being drawn for a "War of the Worlds" —

between the real world of nature and the fantasy worlds of our digital fashioning. He considers the enthusiasm digital technologies engender by their ability to create a world — cyberspace — that has no necessary connection to physical reality to be as distasteful as Augustine's radical preference for the soul over the body.

This criticism of the dualism of the digital media strikes a responsive chord among contemporary theologians, especially those influenced by feminism and by the environmental movement, who have seen the traditional soul-body dualism as the source of both the patriarchalism of classical theology and the view that human dominion over creation justifies human exploitation and misuse of the natural world. Thus Rosemary Ruether has shown how Augustine's dualism masks a sexual politics which justifies the domination of women by men. Sally McFague has identified that same dualism as the source of Christian abuse of the natural world. At a time when contemporary theologians have stressed the importance of the body, of the role of the natural world in sacramental and incarnational theologies, this apparent reversion by digital technology to a discredited dualism and disrespect for the body is regarded with suspicion.

It is important that we not idealize the role of the body in communication. It is true that in a face-to-face encounter between two people, a good deal of information is exchanged that is absent in more remote types of communication. We often receive the greatest support from other people in the form of touch or glance. As communication is removed further and further from physical presence, we seem to impoverish what truly human communication can be. But that is not the whole story. Physical presence, the body, can also inhibit communication. Physical presence can sometimes be intimidating. We use our body, or parts of it, to miscommunicate. We can domineer over someone with our size, or by the way we use our eyes. Conversely, we can be cowed into silence by physical proximity. Sometimes communication is served by physical distance.

In order to appreciate the promise of digital technology for communication, it is important to avoid the temptation of becoming "metaphysical" about what digital technology does. The virtual reality enthusiast who rhapsodizes over the escape from mundane physical existence promised by the new media turns these digitally created worlds into a kind of transcendent heavenly realm. At the opposite pole, a Mark Slouka (who is quite sure that the world of physical nature alone is "real") adopts, whether he admits it or not, an extreme metaphysical materialism which in the end must deny any relationship between imagination and reality, which has no place for worlds of the spirit.

Hypertext and worlds of the imagination

In allowing us to construct worlds of imagination, digital technology is not different from the traditional arts of painting, sculpture, story-telling. Where the difference comes is in the degree to which it can, given enough bandwidth, surround us by and immerse us in an imaginary world. It can do this in ways traditional arts can only hint at. Since it is not confined to a single medium, digital technology can simultaneously engage our eyes, ears and touch. Graphics, sounds and text can be combined in a single presentation.

Let us consider the power of digital technology solely from the perspective of text. We encountered the concept of hypertext in chapter 2 when we considered the World Wide Web. Hypertext allows one to move from a word or phrase in one document to a quite different document which will give more information about that word or phrase. In hypertext one can jump from point to point and not necessarily ever return to the point from which one started.

Traditional text is linear. That is, in a document or a book one is expected generally to start at the beginning and continue through until one reaches the end. In fact, text is rarely used in quite that way. Often I will take a book from the shelf, look at its index or table of contents, then go directly to the page with the information I am looking for. Or, when reading an essay, my eyes will be drawn by a footnote to the bottom of a page. The footnote may direct me to an essay in another book, which I may then pull from my shelf to consult. I jump from footnote to footnote, perhaps never returning to the essay from which I started.

Devices like tables of contents, indexes and footnotes are all ways in which traditional texts have tried to become hypertextual. A similar point could be made in regard to that quality of traditional texts that has often been called "intertextuality" — the way in which a text can allude to other texts, inviting us to make an imaginative jump by recalling these texts.

The Bible itself can be seen as a text that wants to be hypertextual. Throughout the biblical text we find allusions to other biblical texts. Time after time the Bible points to itself in hypertextual ways. Many printed Bibles put notes in the margins or at the bottom of the page which direct the reader to other passages to which particular verses point.

In the Sermon on the Mount, for example, Jesus' words point us again and again to passages in the Hebrew scriptures: "You have heard that it is said…" We are asked to make a hypertextual leap in our own minds to the commandments: "Thou shalt not kill", "Thou shalt not commit adultery". Again, when Paul speaks in the Letter to the Romans of Christ as the "second Adam", we are invited mentally to jump to the text of Genesis 2-3. The imagery of the book of Revelation invites those who know the Hebrew scriptures to jump to the text of the book of Daniel. Over and over the Bible strains towards hypertextuality.

Because the Bible has a beginning and an end — because it begins with *the* Beginning and ends with *the* End — we may be tempted to think of its content and message as something linear. In fact, it is only relatively recently in the history of the Judaeo-Christian tradition that most believers have come to experience the Bible as something linear. In the history of the reception of the Bible, most believers have encountered the word of the Bible not in its linear dimensions but as episodic, as the succession of readings from week to week in synagogue or church, as a cyclical story repeated anew in each liturgical year. Even those relatively few believers who encountered the Bible as text — as the written or printed word — often had it only in the form of isolated passages or as a collection of scrolls. The Bible as a codex, as a bound book with a definite beginning and a definite end, is only one form that the sacred text has assumed in the history of its transmission.

Considering a text as something linear attributes a kind of objectivity to it, an "out-thereness". We start at the beginning, follow a well-defined path and end up with a definite conclusion. We can trace the course of a text in a way analogous to the way we trace out a route on a map. Both a map and a linear text protect us from getting lost by externalizing the route that we are to follow.

Electronic hypertexts, by contrast, may or may not have a "beginning" — in the sense of a standard point of entry to the text. It would be possible, however, to design an electronic hypertext which a reader entered at a random point generated by the computer. The paradigmatic hypertext of our time, the World Wide Web, has no standard entry point. The reader chooses for himself or herself where to begin. But whether or not there is a beginning, once one is inside a hypertext, there is certainly no standard route to the end. Indeed, there may well not be any definite end other than the point at which the reader chooses to end the exploration. (But here we must make the qualification that many hypertexts today are basically printed texts which have been transferred to an electronic medium with a few electronic links added to them. The habits of print die hard.) In a hypertext, the reader chooses which links to follow. The author cannot predict the route that any given reader will take. Reading a hypertext is more like immersing oneself in a textual world where one can explore than like tracing a route from point A to point B on a map. Rather than the sense of objectivity we get from printed texts, a hypertext has the ability metaphorically to wrap itself around the reader, to create an environment within which the reader is able to move with relative freedom.

The World Wide Web, which was originally designed as a means for networks of scientists to locate information on the Internet in a simpler way, has become the standard way for most people to engage the Internet today. As the Web has grown, Web browsers like Netscape Navigator and Microsoft's Internet Explorer have integrated the ability to do things like exchanging electronic mail and reading Usenet newsgroups into their capabilities. In this way, the World Wide Web has effectively transformed the Internet into a global hypertext.

"Surfing the Net" can then be seen as a paradigmatic way of reading hypertext. As a global hypertext, the Internet has no beginning or end. It is not "about" anything. It is a world — cyberspace — that is there for our exploration. To enter into this text, then, is to surround ourselves with it, to let it be the environment in which we move. Every reading of this text is different. Heraclitus's maxim that one cannot step into the same river twice applies to reading a hypertext like the Web.

I think it can be argued that a religious community uses its sacred texts more like a hypertext than like a book. One occasionally encounters a person who has read the Bible through from beginning to end, from Genesis 1 to Revelation 22. People make a point of mentioning this precisely because it is *not* the way the Bible is normally used. The Bible is used in many different ways in Christian communities, but its use as a "book" may well be the exception rather than the rule in the history of its transmission from its beginnings to the Bible of today.

Perhaps it is more adequate to see a sacred text like the Bible as constructing a world in which the believer is initiated and in which he or she is expected to live. The sacred text constructs a world of the imagination which I as a believer enter, explore and inhabit. Through the liturgy, the preaching of the church, devotional reading and disciplined study, I jump from place to place in that world, continually making new connections, discovering new links, entering more and more deeply into the world of the sacred text. In other words, in a living religious community a sacred text is used more like a hypertext, even if it takes the physical form, as the Bible usually does today, of a printed book.

5. Sinning in Cyberspace

Democracy, anarchy and the net

In our exploration of information technology thus far, we have mentioned some of the negative aspects of the digital revolution. We have noted some of the ambiguities of the changes digital technology has produced in the contemporary world. As with any change, the digitization of the world carries both promise and threat, both gain and loss. While attempting to be reasonably even-handed in describing the impact of digital technology, we have not yet addressed some of the more objectionable features associated with cyberspace in the public mind: the ready availability of online pornography, the use of the Internet by hate groups or terrorists or the phenomenon of online crime.

Neither the appearance of pornography and hate literature nor the new opportunities for criminal gain made possible by computer networks should come as a surprise. After all, if as we have said the computer is a possibility machine, then we should expect that even the possibilities that are represented by pornography, hate literature and criminal activity will find a place in the digital reality that is cyberspace. If salvation has to do with the ultimate meaning of human life and the over-coming of alienation and the powers of death, then it must be said emphatically that digital technology does not promise us salvation. Digital technology may provide us with new pos-sibilities of speed and accuracy. It may overcome earlier limits set to human self-expression by barriers of space and time. But the ambivalences of the human heart will not be abolished by the new medium. If anything, it enables us to do our sinning in new, faster and more efficient ways.

In many ways, digital technology introduces us to a world for which many have longed. Traditional hierarchical forms of social organization have developed, at least in part, from the limitations that space and time have imposed on human society and commerce. Civilization as we know it has been made possible because certain centres have been able to impose an order on certain margins. Without hierarchical control, many of the benefits of civilization would not have come about. For example, the ability of the Roman empire to ensure the safety of trade routes around the Mediterranean and on the European continent made a certain material standard of living possible under the *Pax Romana*. With the decline of central power, Western Europe entered the period we often call the "dark ages". In that context, another form of hierarchy, known as the feudal system, allowed local communities to survive and protect themselves in a situation which could otherwise have been described as anarchy. With the re-emergence of central authorities, with the growth of the power of monarchies, the growth of commerce laid the material basis for the flowering of culture in the high middle ages.

New hierarchies have often replaced older ones. In modern times, the hierarchy of capital has tended to replace the traditional hierarchy of land tenure. The hierarchy of representative democracy has tended to replace the hierarchy of the aristocracy. New hierarchies have appeared — colonialisms, bureaucracies, hierarchies of language and race. In each case, a relatively few make decisions for the many.

Under the impact of liberation theology and feminist theology, hierarchical structures have recently been subject to intensive criticism in the church. Indeed, one might get the impression from much contemporary theology that hierarchy and the domination of the many by the few constitute the original sin of humanity. In place of hierarchical control, consensual, participatory decision-making processes are commended.

Against this background digital technology may seem to offer a bright promise. In digitally mediated communities, distributed decision-making is encouraged. In a hierarchy, information flows up from the "grassroots" to the top from where it is redistributed to the "grassroots". Or, to use another metaphor, information in hierarchical systems flows from the margins to the centre where it is distributed to the margins. Hierarchical structures exercise considerable power by virtue of their ability to control the flow of information.

With computer communication, hierarchical systems can be completely bypassed in the distribution of information. As a user of the Internet, I can send information, with minimal effort and expense, to a great number of individuals who may be located in places that are very distant from me. If I put up a Web page, for example, anyone interested in the information I have to offer can have instant access to it. I do not need to send it to an administrative centre to be included in their next bulk mailing. I do not need to depend on any gatekeepers, in the form of bureaucratic structures or in the form of the mass media, to package my information in a way that will allow it to reach its intended audience. In short, computer communication marginalizes hierarchy.

Is that good news or bad news? Actually, it is both. With a medium like e-mail or the World Wide Web, the ability to publish, to attract an audience, is available to anyone with the requisite technology — a computer and modem. In an age of technological disparity, that does not quite add up to equality but, when compared to other media, the access of the individual to the information one needs and the ability to publish whatever one chooses is remarkably enhanced. In online communication, the hierarchical dimensions of the medium are usually well hidden.

Some remnants of hierarchical organization do exist in the online world. If I want access to the Internet, I have two choices. My first choice would be to become my own Internet provider and thus have virtually complete control of my Internet access. I would set up a server (the software that allows me to connect to the Internet and to use its protocols) and arrange for direct connection to the Internet.

To do this, however, would be very expensive. Moreover, not only would I have to pay hundreds of dollars a month for a direct connection to the Internet. I would also have to spend considerable time in learning many of the technical details of Internet servers which an ordinary Internet user does not need to know. It is much cheaper, in time and in money, to purchase my access to the Internet from another provider whose costs will be distributed over hundreds of other customers like me.

When I purchase access from an Internet provider, however, I give up considerable control. My Internet provider will allow me access to certain Internet features, probably offer certain other features for an extra charge and may not offer other features at all. Can I have my own Web page? Yes — but usually this will mean an extra fee. When I connect to the Internet through my provider, I am in effect enclosed in a "shell" which allows me to use only those Internet features that my provider will allow. If I were my own provider, I could configure my access any way I chose. As a user of someone else's service, I am subject to certain powers which the operators of that service have. This is the hierarchy of the online world.

To the inhabitant of the virtual world of the Internet, this hierarchical aspect is often hidden or irrelevant. If I have contracted for the service, I can, at little cost, publish a Web page. I can publicize my page on services like Yahoo, which are consulted by Internet users all over the world, making my page readily available to anyone looking for the kind of material I have published. I have virtually the same access to the medium as the publishers of *Time* or the *Wall Street Journal* or the Disney organization. On the Internet, I can start my own "Zine" (online magazine) or moderate my own discussion group.

It all sounds very democratic. In fact, what is happening has little to do with democracy. Democracy is rule by the people. In a democracy, I am subject to the will of the majority as represented by those whom "the people" have chosen to exercise power on their behalf. Even in very small democracies, I am subject to the will of the group. The fact that I can participate to a greater or lesser degree in the democratic decision-making process does not absolve me from abiding by laws with which I may personally disagree. Democracy does not abolish hierarchy.

The opposite to hierarchy is not democracy. The opposite to hierarchy is anarchy. The so-called "dark ages" of Western Europe are a case in point. What made those ages "dark" was the inability of any central authority to preserve the structures of "civilization" during that period. Hierarchy — whether democratic or authoritarian — has the benefit of providing a modicum of order which allows community to function.

This is not to say that anarchy is unambiguously undesirable. Like hierarchy, anarchy has its good points and its bad points. The rough equality of access to the Internet allows a flourishing of self-expression at a level that has rarely if ever been seen in human society. The negative side of this is that some of these forms of self-expression are obscene, filled with hate and even illegal. In anarchy, by definition, there is no ruler, no *archon,* with the power to enforce community standards, to curb illegal behaviour.

According to a hacker slogan, "Information wants to be free". In civilized society, however, it has always been possible to place limits on human freedom. I am not free, for example, to behave in a way that infringes on the basic rights of others in society. My freedom is limited by the rights of others and often by the vital interests of the community in which I live. In cyberspace, we are currently faced with the question of whether there should be limits on the freedom of information especially in three areas: pornography, hate propaganda and privacy.

Online pornography

In July 1996 a court in San Jose, California, indicted 16 men on charges of online pornography and child molestation. Of the 16, three were known only by a pseudonym and in fact lived outside the United States. All were members of a group which called itself the Orchid Club. They had been meeting for some time in cyberspace where they exchanged their experiences of paedophilia and often chatted as one of their members engaged in child molestation while describing the experience for the other members of the "club".

The existence of the Orchid Club came to light only because of that part of their activity which did not take place in cyberspace. A six-year-old child reported to her parents the strange behaviour of the father of a friend at whose home she had been visiting. As a result of this incident, and the willingness of some members of the club to cooperate with police, the ring of paedophiles was exposed and the indictments issued.

This story, carried by the world press, reinforces the fears of many parents about cyberspace. If a child has access to the Internet, what will he or she find there? Will children seek out or stumble upon graphic sexual scenes? Will they encounter someone who will subject them to a virtual seduction? Can the Internet be made safe for children? Can certain kinds of material not be banned from cyberspace?

These fears are not without substance. Pornographic materials are available online for those who seek them out. It is possible, when surfing the Web, to stumble on something you would prefer not to see. It may be the pornography of sex. It may be the pornography of violence. It may be the pornography of hate. Whatever brand of pornography one may think of, it can be found somewhere online.

The US Congress attempted to deal with the availability of online pornography by passing the Communications Decency Act, which was signed into law by President Clinton in February 1996. It provided a penalty of two years in prison and a $250,000 fine for anyone who made pornography or other objectionable material available over the Internet.

This legislation was vigorously opposed by many groups who claimed to represent the interests of Internet providers and users. They argued that the act would contravene constitutional guarantees of the freedom of speech, and they raised serious questions about how well the legislators understood the new technology represented by the Internet and the World Wide Web. The new law treated Internet "publishing" as if it were analogous to the mass media: print and broadcasting. In fact, those opposing it argued, the new technology is distinctly different.

Some of those opponents challenged the constitutionality of the Communications Decency Act; and in June 1996, an injunction against its enforcement was issued by a panel of three judges in Philadelphia. The judges had undergone what *The New York Times* described as a "crash course" before issuing the injunction, and a columnist described their judgment as "one of the most lucid primers about the Internet yet seen". The judges held that the Internet was a "wholly unique medium" that could not be reasonably compared to broadcasting. Regarding the provision making it an offence to make certain materials available to children, one judge argued that since there is no way an Internet "publisher" could ascertain the age of those who accessed their materials, these providers were left with the choice between silence and the risk of prosecution. Another judge, Steward Dalzell, wrote:

> Some of the dialogue on the Internet surely tests the limits of conventional discourse. Speech on the Internet can be unfiltered, unpolished and unconventional, even emotionally charged, sexually explicit and vulgar — in a word "indecent" in many communities. But we should expect such speech to occur in a medium in which citizens from all walks of life have a voice. We should also protect the autonomy that such a medium confers to ordinary people as well as media magnates (cited in *The New York Times*, 13 June 1996).

The debate over pornography on the Internet is in many senses simply a continuation of the ongoing debate over free speech in society. Ought there to be limits on the freedom of expression for the sake of the welfare of the community as a whole? In free and open democratic societies, this debate has usually been resolved by the recognition of minimal limits to the types of expression that can be legitimately pursued. In the case of pornography, however, the question of what constitute "minimal limits" elicits considerable difference of opinion, according to culture, religious belief, geographical location, social class, educational level and a host of other variables.

In the United States, courts have often ruled on questions of the censorship of pornographic literature by reference to something called "local standards". In cyberspace, however, a reference to "local standards" only complicates the issue, for in cyberspace there is no "here". This was clearly illustrated by a case in which the operator of a BBS in the state of California was successfully prosecuted in the state of Tennessee for the distribution of pornographic material in Tennessee. An undercover law enforcement officer from Memphis, Tennessee, called the BBS and downloaded pornographic material; and on that basis the California BBS operator was charged, under Tennessee law, with violating the local standards of Memphis.

Note that this incident did not take place on the Internet. The Tennessee officer called the California BBS by long distance and deliberately chose what to download. It could be argued that it was the officer, not the BBS operator, who brought the offending material into Tennessee. However, since the material was freely available to any resident of Tennessee by calling the California BBS, the operator was convicted for distributing material that was obscene according to Memphis community standards.

But why should Tennessee standards apply to a California information provider? Does this conviction not imply that the community with the narrowest standards and the most restrictive censorship laws will govern what is legal or not in cyberspace? Is a BBS operator obligated to know the local laws of a caller's community before giving access to him or her?

On the Internet, however, the problems are even more complicated. On the World Wide Web, I do not necessarily know where the document I am looking at comes from. Sometimes I get a clue to its location from its URL (Web address), but often not even that gives me much information about the geographical location of the computer on which the document is stored. In a sense, everything on the Web is *here*, connected to my computer screen by a button, an icon or a "hot spot" on the screen. From my point of view, everything on the Internet is on my computer.

In this situation, what happens to "community standards"? It will be possible for me, as an individual, to "black out" some of the things I do not want to see or want my children to see. But I cannot black out everything, and there is almost always a way around any limits I try to impose on anyone who uses my computer. If I am an Internet access provider, I may want to limit the things that can be accessed through my service, but if I refuse to carry the "alt.sex" newsgroups on Usenet, my users can always telnet to a service that does carry them. And who is to prevent a Memphis Internet user from downloading materials that are banned in Memphis from a site in Amsterdam?

Of course, these technical and legal problems do not arise only with pornography; and in the next section we shall look more closely at another type of material that many people find objectionable. In cyberspace, "there is no king, and all the people do what is right in their own eyes" (Judg. 21:25).

The alarm expressed by defenders of free speech over attempts to impose limits on the Internet is not because they want to justify pornography or hate literature. The problem that concerns the many libertarians of the Net is that those who attempt to impose "community standards" on the Net do not understand the technology and will end up by destroying this marvellous new resource through misguided legislation. On the other hand, many people feel that some forms of expression — particularly pornography, hate propaganda, libel, slander — cause harm and must be subject to legal sanctions. Each side is able to present its point of view through the Internet. Neither, however, is able to impose it as the law of cyberspace.

Virtual hate

The use of the Internet to promote hatred has generally received less attention in the public press than the availability of pornographic materials, although online hate propaganda raises concerns that may be even more troubling. There are Web sites devoted to "the preservation of the white race", usually from the threat of Jewish conspiracies or the "mongrelization" of society (which is typically seen on these sites as a Jewish conspiracy). There is material attacking gays and lesbians, Roman Catholics, immigrants, etc., etc.

Since 1991, Kenneth McVay has devoted his energies to exposing hate groups on the Internet. McVay's Web site, the Nitzkor Project (http://www.Nitzkor.org), has documented the online activities of hate groups, particularly anti-semitic and "holocaust denial" Web sites. According to McVay the Internet provides hate groups with a potential audience — about 70 million — to which they would not normally have access. More dangerous than sites whose rhetoric of hatred is blatant, says McVay, are those which maintain a veneer of respectability and use academic and rational-sounding discourse to promote their hostility, for the casual Web surfer will be much more easily swayed by the lies of the hate propaganda presented in a respectable, even academic style. Consequently, he devotes a significant portion of the Nitzkor Project Web sites to documenting the contradictions and answering the untruths and manufactured "facts" that appear in the propaganda of racist sites.

But we must remember that the Internet is not like broadcasting. Ernst Zündel is a so-called "holocaust denier" who has achieved a certain notoriety in Germany and in Canada (where he presently lives). When Zündel is in the news, as he was when he was charged with violating Canada's hate laws, he appears frequently in clips on news broadcasts on Canadian television. If such a clip includes a "sound bite" of Zündel, he has a guaranteed audience on the nightly news of Canada's two television networks of several million. Although this is considerably short of the 70 million McVay estimates is available on the Internet, it is misleading to compare the *potential* audience on the Internet with the *actual* audience on television. The potential audience for the nightly television news in Canada is arguably in the range of 20 million — the number of Canadians with access to television — and if CNN picks up the Canadian clip, as it sometimes does for its international cable news system, the potential audience for Zündel's sound bite leaps into the hundreds of millions.

How large is the audience for hate literature on the Internet? The answer in the case of Zündel is not readily available, since his Web site does not use a counter (which shows how many times a site has been accessed). But some of Zündel's anti-semitic colleagues do. The Committee for Open Debate on the Holocaust (CODOH), which McVay numbers among the more dangerous sites because of its apparent appeal to "open debate", shows around 20,000 accesses in about 11 months. "The Aryan Crusader's Library", which includes links to a great number of anti-semitic sites, shows 34,000 accesses in an undefined period as of September 1996. "Stormfront", described by the *Web Review* as "the pre-eminent site of its kind", shows 315,000 accesses in a year-and-a-half.

What are we to make of those figures? On the one hand, even CODOH's 20,000 accesses would seem to be more than the group could reach by printed literature in a same period. But we have no idea how many individual people these accesses represent. For example, a hard core of 300 supporters around the world who accessed "Stormfront" daily would account for more than half of the site's total accesses. In any case, the 315,000 accesses that "Stormfront" boasts over a year-and-a-half is far short of the millions reached by Zündel with a sound bite on one night's news.

There is another important difference between Zündel on the news and Zündel on the World Wide Web. If I am watching the nightly news, as I usually do, I have little choice but to hear what Zündel has to say when his clip appears. On the Web, I am unlikely to encounter Zündel unless I go looking for him. Without my active cooperation, the fact that Zündel has a Web page does not intrude itself on my use of the Web. Although it is not impossible, it is rare that anyone would stumble on Zündel's Web site who was not looking for information relating to anti-semitism and the holocaust.

If the audience for racist propaganda on the Web is limited, does that mean that there is little cause for concern?

Not at all. What information technology gives the racist fringes of society is the same thing it gives other groups: connectivity. The Internet allows these groups — the holocaust deniers, the white supremacists, the militia movements in the US — to be in touch, to build on each other's work, to create a web of hate that festers under the apparently benign surface of computer networks. It is a power that is not insignificant.

Is legislation against the propagation of hate on the Internet possible? Some would like to believe it is. The *Web Review* quotes Rabbi Abraham Cooper of the Simon Wiesenthal Centre as criticizing the notion that the Internet should be a "free market-place of ideas". He observes that "there is a difference between the Flat Earth Society and Carl Sagan... The Internet can give the erroneous impression that all information is of the same value." The problem here is the apparent assumption that there exists some perspective from which it can be determined what is valuable information and what is not and that it would be desirable and ought to be possible to impose these determinations. This repeats the assumption of the Roman Catholic magisterium prior to the Second Vatican Council that "error has no rights". Such an assumption, whether in modern liberal garb, or Islamic fundamentalist garb, or in Tridentine Catholic garb, or in Nazi garb, opens a Pandora's box. While it might provide a justification for banning hate literature from the Web, it would also provide a justification for banning much more.

The practicality of such censorship is something else. It is possible to place limits on what can be said in a free and open society as long as some person or group (like a national government) is able to exercise sovereignty. Cyberspace, as we have already observed, is extra-national. It evades any attempt to control it.

Ken McVay's Nitzkor Project may indeed represent the only viable strategy for countering hate propaganda that is possible in cyberspace. In effect, he attempts to expose the literature of the holocaust deniers to the light of day, to counter the disinformation of these groups with the information of the outsider, to break the reinforcement of the incestuous links that bind one hate site to another. In effect he is using the openness of the Internet as a weapon against those who appeal to its openness as a legitimation of their Internet presence.

Privacy online

In the novel and film *The Pelican Brief*, a young law student is forced to flee some powerful people whose complicity in several assassinations she has uncovered. She soon discovers that her enemies are able to follow her through the trail of credit card transactions she leaves. It can be very difficult in contemporary life to avoid creating a data trail that can in principle be followed by those powerful enough or influential enough to gain access to those data.

Every time we venture into cyberspace we leave a data trail. I must assume that when I log on to the Internet through my Internet provider, a record is kept of the time of my call and of how long I am online. I must also assume that traces of my online activities are spread throughout the Internet: what Web sites I visit, what files I download, what services I use, what mailing lists I subscribe to, what people I have sent e-mail and received e-mail from me in return.

Furthermore, I must assume that in principle the various data trails I leave by my online activities, my credit card transactions, my travel reservations, my investments and my telephone calls could all be collected and related to each other. That is to say, there is an immense amount of information about me in computer data banks throughout the world. Some of the most intimate details of my life are "out there", in cyberspace. These may be located in thousands of different, unconnected data bases, but under certain conditions much of this information *could* be gathered in a single report.

Besides the possibility of tracing my data trail, the other contemporary threat to my privacy from computer technology is that of having my private communications intercepted by people or institutions to whom I do not wish to give access to the information in those communications. This threat may take the form of someone learning my credit card number from a transaction I make online, or a government security agency could be routinely reading my mail.

Both these types of threat to privacy are real in the sense of representing capabilities within the range of existing technology. It is technologically possible to follow the data trail I leave every time I go online. Similarly, it is possible to follow the data trail I leave in the computer data banks of the world when I use my bank card at the local supermarket, pay for a purchase with a credit card, make a phone call, negotiate a loan and so on. Similarly, it is technologically possible that my e-mail could be intercepted or my credit card number stolen online.

In fact, I do not lie awake at night fretting about these possibilities. I can think of no conceivable reason why anyone would want to know about my online activity and I do not worry that someone somewhere may be tracking my credit card purchases to construct a profile of my buying habits. Some of these things may be happening, but I doubt it; and whatever information anyone may have gathered from my online activity has not resulted in any harm to me, as far as I can tell.

It seems to me that the mass media magnify the risks to privacy through online activities in relation to other threats. True, a programme called a "sniffer" could extract my credit card number from one of my online transactions. But the number could also be overheard if my telephone line were tapped, or it could be discovered from my monthly bill by someone with access to my mail. Indeed, my impression is that problems with the postal service are a greater source of credit card fraud than are online transactions.

Who are those who would threaten my privacy? For the most part, the threat does not come from individuals who I meet online. I consider myself a sophisticated computer user. I understand how computers work. I can write computer programmes in several languages. I can usually find my way around strange computer systems. However, I have no idea about how to write a "sniffer" programme, nor would I be able to get access to the many places where vital information about others is stored. I would not know how to intercept someone else's mail. The threat to online privacy does not come from someone like me.

Who would have the knowledge and power to access private information about me? Basically, the threat comes from four possible sources: (1) hackers, that is people who make it their business to understand computers so thoroughly that they can do things far beyond the ordinary user and to whom every computer system is a new challenge; (2) system operators, that is, those who run the computer systems on which my data is stored; (3) big business, that is, those who have the money and the motivation to go to the expense and effort of gathering information about me; and (4) government, usually in the interest of law and order or national security. Let us consider each threat in turn.

One morning when I logged on to the Internet I was informed that my password had been cancelled. I had to phone my provider and furnish evidence that I was who I claimed to be so that I could be given a new password. The reason for this was that the university computers I used had been subject to an attack by a hacker, who had penetrated the system and actually obtained the file with all the passwords. This meant that, in principle, nothing on the system would be protected from the hacker's gaze.

The incident illustrates that, while I find it incredulous that some anonymous hacker is interested in targeting me for attack, my privacy is vulnerable if the systems I use are vulnerable. Most hackers are not malicious: they are interested in the challenge of defeating the security system rather than in the illicit use of information they might obtain in the process. But my interest in the security of my communications is related to the total security of the system I use.

As for my vulnerability to a system operator, I must trust in the integrity of the systems I use. Anyone who has ever operated a bulletin board system will know that this gives one access to anything that any user may post there. This is not to say that a BBS operator reads everything on the system, but that capability is there. In a well-run system, only a few people will have accounts with wide-ranging access to information anywhere on the system; and such accounts may be reserved for emergency use only. But a user of computer systems should be aware that this capability always exists and act accordingly. Generally, I cannot imagine what interest a system operator would have in my mail. However, if I am paranoid or if I am communicating particularly sensitive information, I will take steps to protect my communications from even accidental interception.

While it is true that big business may have an interest in data about me, I know that credit agencies and other enterprises in the information business have ways of getting that information quite independently of my online activities. This is not to deny that the availability of private information to business is a matter of concern, but only that it is not unique to cyberspace.

The issues surrounding the threat to privacy from government are well illustrated by the "Clipper chip" debate.

It is widely recognized that the answer to many of the online privacy concerns is encryption. That is, if all my communications were in a virtually unbreakable code, I would have no reason to fear the gaze of hackers or system operators, big business or government. If all my online mail were coded messages that the system operator could not read, I would have no reason to fear his or her power.

However, this capability would require a very good code. In fact, codes do exist that are virtually impossible to break. They are produced by a method known as "public key" encryption (a "key" is a formula followed by a coding programme in producing a coded text; the longer it is, the more difficult the code will be to break). These systems use two keys: one is a "private" key, which only I know, the other a "public" key, which anyone may know. Someone wanting to send me a secure message can use my public key to produce the coded message, but thereafter only the private key, the one that I alone know, can decode the message. Not even the person who originally sent the message can decode it.

There are a number of public key encryption systems in existence. That would seem to solve the problem. If everyone encrypted online data, there would be no threat to privacy.

Enter the United States government. The government has two concerns. The first, inherited from the cold war, is that its own encryption systems should not be available to the nation's "enemies". Thus it has been against the law to export highly secure encryption technology from the US, which has meant that any coded communication across international borders could be done only with inferior, breakable encryption systems.

In the early 1990s a computer programmer with an interest in cryptology and a commitment to the rights of computer users to privacy created an encryption system called PGP ("Pretty Good Privacy") and released it into the public domain. The result is that, despite US government policy, a secure encryption system has been widely distributed internationally.

This raises the second concern of government. Traditionally, the government has always claimed the right, under certain more or less clearly defined circumstances, to intercept private communications: to open mail or to tap telephones when criminal activities or threats to national security are suspected. However, if computer communications were virtually impossible to decode, this would provide a communication medium par excellence for organized crime and international terrorism.

The government's solution was the "Clipper chip". This was a chip that would be built into every computer and encrypt all of its communication, assuring every computer user nearly secure communications. The word "nearly" was the problem. The government would require that the private key of anyone using the Clipper chip would be held by an agency which would release it only to government investigators and only under a court order. In this way, the government argued, computer communications would be secure enough while the government's ability to ensure public security would not be compromised.

At the time of writing, the Clipper chip appears to be a dead issue, although the US government still wishes to press the concerns for national security against the uncompromising "freedom of speech" concerns of privacy advocates. In the meantime, most computer communications are not encrypted and are, therefore, vulnerable in principle to unauthorized interception. It is safe to say that improved and easier-to-use encryption methods will continue to be developed. Whether complete privacy online will ever be secured remains an open question.

6. Living in Virtual Un/Reality

The "virtually" real

The term "virtual reality" was coined to describe the computer's ability to simulate or create a reality of its own. "Virtual reality" devices enable us to substitute sensual information generated by the computer for our sensual contact with the external world. Thus, by donning goggles, earphones and gloves which are connected to a computer, I can have the experience of being in a different world: a world which has no existence outside the computer that generates the images conveyed to me through this special equipment.

It should be clear by now, however, that the computer generates "worlds" in some very different ways. Most of these worlds I can enter without masking out the external world that my senses perceive. I do not have a pilot's licence, but through my computer and Microsoft's Flight Simulator I have gone island-hopping in a simulated Caribbean. I have visited the enchanted world of *Myst* while sitting at my own disk. When I log on to Ecunet to read the notes in the various discussions there, I converse with a different world of people from that of my day-to-day contacts in my neighbourhood or work-place. To log on to Ecunet is like visiting a coffee house that exists nowhere but in cyberspace which is frequented by people I know, many of whom have become old friends. As I enter each of these worlds, however, I am completely aware that I remain sitting at my desk in front of my computer.

We must think of "virtual reality" in a sense beyond that of the mere substitution of computer-generated data for sensory information. When we speak here of "virtual reality", we are thinking in the broadest sense of the ability of computer to construct and simulate worlds. Included in "virtual reality" is also the world of a Windows desktop or even an ordinary spreadsheet. Through the computer we create a space which is not a space, a world in which we can act and react. In "virtual reality" we include all the worlds we enter when we turn on a computer.

The programming of reality

In the first chapter of Genesis, we read a story of reality. The image behind the story is of God as an omnipotent ruler whose very word is law. God speaks and it is done. So God says, "Let there be light", and there *is* light. In response to God's word, reality happens. Nothing intervenes between the word of God and reality. God speaks. Reality happens.

Now let us change the image. Instead of an omnipotent ruler issuing commands, let us think of God as a divine computer programmer, sitting at a keyboard. God types, "Light", and light happens. God types, "Separate light, darkness", and it happens. And as the divine computer programme is run, light happens, water happens, dry land happens, vegetation happens, animals happen, humanity happens.

Many Christians will feel uncomfortable with that image. To suggest that we could make Genesis 1 more relevant by thinking of God as a computer programmer rather than as a heavenly king may sound tacky and trivial. Nevertheless, let us dwell on this image for a little while. Let us play with the image of God as a computer programmer in order to help us think about reality.

Many people who have done computer programming are familiar with a God-like feeling that comes from the power computers place in our hands. In programming a computer, we create worlds. We type, and it happens. We bring worlds into being *ex nihilo* — out of nothing.

But what have we created? When we programme a computer, what we create is a series of messages. Yet the series of messages — the commands we give the computer — are not the worlds we create. The worlds we create are what happens when our programmes are run on the computer and the computer responds to our messages, when our messages take life through the magic of a central processing unit.

As computer programmers, we are very conscious of the transience of our creations. We run our programmes. Reality happens. And yet when we turn off our computers, the reality is gone. The physical traces of our programme, the magnetic signals on our hard disk which we call a "file", is not the reality. What resides on the hard disk is not the world we created. The file on the disk is only the way we freeze our messages so that we can reissue our commands again later without having to retype them. Our programmes are a reality that happens in response to our commands. When our commands are given, a reality comes into being, only to disappear into nothingness when the computer is turned off, or even when we exit our programme.

The reality we inhabit when we use a computer is a reality brought into being by the commands of a programmer. Most of the programmes we use are the work of someone else. But if I turn on a Mac, or load Windows on a PC, or even when I use good old DOS, I enter a world that has been brought into being by the word of some programmer or programmers. Their messages, frozen on disk or burned into ROM, create that world — the strange reality we have come to call cyberspace.

The analogy between the creation story of Genesis 1 and the experience of computer programmes is thus not so far-fetched. Reality happens in response to the word of God. The world that happens in response to the word of the programmer we have begun to call "virtual reality".

We may well be uncomfortable with the suggestion that we create worlds out of nothing when we turn on the computer. We know how transient the worlds of our creation are. They are made out of bits and bytes. Bits and bytes live, perhaps, in the memory of a computer or on a hard disk. Yet they are not physical. They are not the atoms in the memory chips or on the hard disk. They are messages that just happen to be carried by the atoms. Our stored messages, our words, bring these worlds into being; and when we exit our programmes, these worlds cease to exist. We want to object that our creations are not reality, but only the ephemeral appearances of reality.

We want our worlds to be solid. But virtual worlds are not solid. There seems to be a difference between the hardware reality that God made and the software reality of our virtual worlds. I know — at least I think I know — that my desk continues to exist when I am not in my office. But does *Myst* exist when I exit the programme? Does the world of the Windows desktop exist when I exit to DOS? A world that is constructed out of our messages does not seem to us to be real. It is, we want to say, the *appearance* of reality. It is, at best, virtual reality. It is virtual un/reality.

It might seem reasonable to distinguish between the hardware worlds, which are really real — solid, stable, permanent — and a software world, which is only apparent — an appearance that is commanded by the messages we send to the computer. Yet if we listen carefully to Genesis 1, it is not quite so reasonable after all. For Genesis 1 suggests that the hardware world, like the software world, is brought into being by the word, the messages, of God. The old idea, first articulated by early Christian writers, that the world is created "out of nothing" should undercut our confidence in the stability of the hardware world. What the early Christian theologians wanted to suggest is that the world has no stability, no solidity, no permanence in itself. The world exists only in and through the word of God, the divine command which summons it into being and without which it would disappear into the nothing from which it came. The more we think about it, the more reality — the world which God has called into being — seems to resemble a world which is created by a computer programme.

The computer and post-modernity

To speak of virtual *un*/reality is not to minimize the importance of the worlds created by our computer software. What I want to call attention to by the slash in "un/reality" is that one of the effects of the daily use of digital technology is the blurring of the sharp distinction between reality and unreality. The *American Heritage Dictionary* defines the word "virtual" as "existing or resulting in essence or effect though not in actual fact, form or name". What this obscure bit of prose means is that a "virtual" something is essentially equivalent to the real thing. In other words, if it looks like a duck, quacks like a duck, waddles like a duck, we may at least say that it is a *virtual* duck. But then, we may ask, how do we tell the difference between a real duck and a virtual duck?

This is not a new problem. The 18th-century philosopher George Berkeley raised doubts about the nature of material reality, arguing that all reality exists in the mind. "To be", Berkeley proposed, "is to be perceived." The real existence of things is not "out there" in some mysterious reality called "matter". To say that a lamp post exists is simply to say that some mind — my mind or the mind of God — perceives a lamp post. The story is told that Samuel Johnson, irritated by what he considered the outrageousness of Berkeley's theory, kicked a lamp post, and declared, "Thus I refute Bishop Berkeley." The problem was of course that Johnson's kick proved nothing. His sore toe was nothing more than just another perception in his mind.

Virtual un/reality is what we have come to call "cyberspace". More and more human beings are coming to inhabit this strange world. It is strange because it is "there" without being there. It is strange because it is constantly shifting, rarely the same from day to day. It is a world of our own making. It is a world that perhaps has some similarity to that of Bishop Berkeley, a world constructed totally of signals or messages existing in those mysterious forms of mind that digital technology has made possible. In cyberspace, "to be is to be digitized".

But let us consider something about how we use the word "real". I have interpreted Genesis 1 as a story about how reality happens. God speaks. Reality happens. But the biblical text goes further and tells us that when reality happens, God pronounces it "good".

What God joins together in Genesis, modern thought has done its best to put asunder. I am referring here to the separation that has been common for centuries in modern thought between "fact" on the one hand and "value" on the other. To the modern mind, the question of fact is a matter of objective truth. Fact is "out there", independent of what I might happen to think about it. Fact is objective. To be objective is to be real. Value on the other hand is not objective. It is arbitrary. Value exists only in the mind of the valuer. Values do not change the facts. Values are subjective. Values are matters of opinion. Values are private concerns. Values are unreal.

Before the scientific revolution — that is, in ancient and mediaeval thought — there was a close connection between fact and value. For the pre-moderns, the highest being and the highest good were identical. Particularly in Western Christian thought, evil was non-being, the absence and the distortion of being. Being and "the Good" were always closely identified. There was no split between fact and value. In Genesis, when God sees reality happen, God sees that it is good. To be real is to be good.

Modern thought has not been quite honest about what it was attempting to do. It is one thing to argue that one cannot derive fact from value or value from fact. It is quite another thing to equate "fact" with reality. For when we suggest that "facts" are "real" but "values" are subjective and not "real", we are already making a *value* judgment. We are using the word "reality" in what could be considered a rather prejudicial way. In order to expel considerations of value, of good and evil, from "reality", we must implicitly pronounce the factual, the objective, to be the Good.

On first encountering the title of this chapter, "Living in Virtual Un/Reality", a reader might think that its purpose is to critique what we normally call "virtual reality". The title might have raised the suspicion that I was going to make a case for considering what we call "virtual reality" inferior to whatever it is we want to claim is *really* "real". The reader might have anticipated the claim would be made that analogue reality is somehow superior to digital reality.

But that is not the purpose of the title. What we need to do, first of all, is to suspect this word "reality". It is a much more slippery word than we usually recognize it to be. We are all products of the modern world. We all share the prejudice that reality is somehow "out there", solid and reliable. What we need to see is that the distinction between "real" reality and virtual reality does not make a lot of sense. Digital technology has called into question our metaphysical prejudices. To dwell in cyberspace is to dwell in a different reality from what modernity has been prepared to admit. To call cyberspace "unreal" is to make a value judgment which, in its own way, exposes the contradiction in the modern enterprise of keeping reality and values rigorously separate.

In recent years, the term "post-modern" has made its way into the vocabulary of philosophy, literary criticism, art and architecture. A constant theme in contemporary cultural criticism, it is not easy to define, for the simple reason that "post-modernism" wears different masks in different contexts.

An important theme in the philosophical discussion of post-modernism relates to what we have been saying about the computer and reality. Post-modern philosophy is highly suspicious of any interpretation of reality that attributes stability, solidity and permanent validity to the worlds of our discourse. Commenting on this convergence of post-modern theory and computer technology, Sherry Turkle argues that the computer has become an object which can represent post-modernity's suspicion of the foundationalism of modernity by involving the computer user in a world constituted by a play of simulacra:

> Post-modernism's objects now exist outside science fiction. They exist in the information and connections of the Internet and the World Wide Web, and in the windows, icons and layers of personal computing. They exist in the creatures on a SimLife computer game, and in the simulations of the quantum world that are routinely used in introductory physics courses. All of these are life on the screen. And with these objects, the abstract ideas... of post-modernism become newly accessible, even consumable (*Life on the Screen*, p.45).

Making the transition

To point to the convergence between information technology and post-modern theory is only to suggest a perspective from which the impact of the computer technology on culture may be viewed. It is not a claim that reality has somehow changed. Rather, it is a suggestion that as we become involved with digital technologies, we experience in ourselves something of the transition that seems to be having an impact on our culture in many different ways. We may react to this transition in a conservative way, drawing apocalyptic visions of what will result from the digitization of the world and appealing, like Mark Slouka, to a romantic, pre-technological vision of reality as the hardware of nature. Conversely, we may react to this transition in a utopian way, somewhat after the manner of *Wired*, the pre-eminent magazine promoting digital culture today. We may see this new, digitized world as offering an answer to all the problems with which modernity has burdened us.

Most of us, however, will not be comfortable with either extreme. We have one foot in modernity and the other in the digital world. As we internalize the new technologies and allow them to inform our vision of reality, there is still within us that which is not quite ready to let go of the values of modernity. We are immigrants. We have been bred in modernity but have been ushered, probably without our consent, into a new land where the certainties, the standards, the rituals of daily life have been altered in obvious and not-so-obvious ways. The rationalization of the world, which modernity persistently equated with "progress", has come up short against the intransigence and revitalization of various fundamentalisms. Universalisms, both religious and secular, have encountered the rise of a stubborn particularism in the guise of resurgent nationalisms. All this is happening at the same time as the world is being wired into what Marshall McLuhan described as the "global village". How is it possible that in a world in which space and time have been decisively conquered by our various information technologies, the result is not a new universalism of the human spirit but the proliferation of particularities? What is this new order into which we are immigrating whether we like it or not?

Communication and the future

The contemporary Italian philosopher Vattimo (*The Transparent Society*, Baltimore, Johns Hopkins Univ. Press) describes the situation of the late 20th century as involving the emergence of a "society of generalized communication". Our time has been marked by the proliferation of communication media, and, he suggests, *everything* has become an object of communication.

Vattimo connects this proliferation of communication with the emergence of pluralism. He remarks on the convergence of the end of colonialism following the second world war and the development of global communication systems. The result of this development — which is one aspect of the technological domination of the world — is that a situation is created in which multiple stories can be told. In modernity — which coincides with the period of Western expansion and the hegemony of Western imperialism — there was one dominant story, one view of history. This view saw history as moving in one direction — that of increasing rationalization, which was called "progress".

The technological domination of the world, in Vattimo's analysis, results in the society of generalized communication. When that happens, however, there can no longer be one dominant and official history. In a society of generalized communication, we may say that the media are hungry for stories. Every story can be told; every story must be told. The paradoxical result of the Western movement towards the rationalization and hence technologization of the world, is that the Western story — the story of rationalization, progress, technological domination — becomes one story among others. Technology has at least this emancipatory effect. We now live in a world of multiple histories.

If we think of the history of the world since the end of the second world war, we can think of many of the new stories which have been told, many of the communities which have newly found a voice: the national stories of Africa and Asia emerging with the dissolution of Western colonial empires; the black community in the United States which could no longer be ignored, at least in part because of media coverage of the civil rights movement; the feminist movement, in which the story of women found its voice; the gay and lesbian movement. Today we are further jolted by the voice of the far right — of those alienated people who form militias in the United States or violently resist non-European immigration into Europe — who are given a voice by the same media. In this process, the political-economic questions of who controls the media and what point of view they represent is not the major factor. Since the media need something to cover, the same media give a voice to whoever it is they cover.

Vattimo has in mind specifically the proliferation of mass media, particularly radio, television, cinema and the press. He does not explicitly address the particular proliferation of communication media with which we have been concerned in this book — although his insight can certainly be extended to it. If the mass media give voice to any and every community, no matter how it is defined, computer communications extends the ability of minorities to speak beyond anything the mass media can muster. On the mass media, according to a famous remark of Andy Warhol, everyone is allotted his or her 15 minutes of fame. That is, even though the mass media are information-hungry, there are limits to what they can carry. If the mass media are caught up in a frenzy over the O.J. Simpson trial or the Olympic games, other voices will have to wait patiently until they too can have their turn. In other words, in the mass media an economy of scarcity still rules. If the media are obsessed with the militia groups, one may nevertheless hope that there are other more positive groups who are not yet being heard.

The Internet is in many ways a paradigm of Vattimo's analysis of the society of generalized communication. In the anarchy of the Internet, every voice can speak. And on the Internet, those who have ears to hear can hear. Every group — whatever its ideology, whatever its commitments — can stake out a corner. Its message can be made available for anyone who wants to search it out or for those who just happen to stumble over it. The pluralization proceeds to the point that everyone can have a Web page, can tell his or her own story, promote his or her own version of the truth for all the world to hear.

We are beginning to realize that a world in which every voice can be heard is not an unmixed blessing. Communication does not always promote understanding. We are discovering that a world in which so many voices can speak is a disquieting and dangerous one. When we free people to speak, we free everyone to speak, even those who represent points of view and commitments we consider inimical to human life and community. As the "end of modernity", as Vattimo calls it, has emancipated us from a single point of view, a single story, a unified version of history, it has also ushered in a world that is chaotic and dangerous. There are some stories we would prefer not to hear, some points of view we would prefer not understand.

Yet that, we may venture to say, is the world into which we have been decisively introduced by the technology we have been celebrating here. In the world of generalized communication, the world in which everything concerns the transmission of messages, we have to discover anew what it means to be church. The models of the past, of the dominance of a single view, will not help us. This is not the world of the *Pax Romana* with all its ambiguities. It is not the world of Christendom, with its benefits and its liabilities. It is not even the world of modernity, of belief in rational progress, and the liberalisms and fundamentalisms it fostered. It is a new world with none of the certainties the church has used to understand its identity in those ages.

None of us can say with any certainty what it means to be church in a society of generalized communication. But a few guesses may be attempted.

1. In a society of generalized communication, any Christian voice will be a multiple voice. The distinction between orthodoxy and heresy will become increasingly problematic.

Of course, the Christian church has always had to deal with the claims of different voices to speak for the gospel. In the world of the *Pax Romana* the church struggled — with only partial success — to ensure that it would speak with a single voice. Particularly in struggling against heresy in the form of gnosticism, it attempted to guarantee that a single, orthodox Christian voice might prevail.

In the world of Christendom, aided by the power of the state, a single official voice did claim to speak in a unitary and definitive way for the church. This was largely successful, especially in Western Europe, where the power of the papacy assured the hegemony of a single Christian voice.

In modernity, the Christian voice was fragmented. Nevertheless, various churches continued to insist either that theirs was the only legitimate Christian voice or that there was a common orthodoxy, shared across at least certain denominational tradition, which constituted *the* authentic and legitimate Christian voice.

In a society of generalized communication, orthodoxy and heresy both have a voice. The very idea of a single authentic Christian voice becomes problematical. Orthodoxy and heresy exist side by side, each insisting on its legitimacy and authenticity. To see that this is already happening, one need only to read online religious discussions, whether in Internet mailing lists or in Ecunet meetings, which make it evident how difficult it is for any single voice to establish itself as normative.

Consider one example. On Ecunet, a meeting called "Confessing Christ" attempted to deal with the problem of the multiplicity of the Christian voice within the United Church of Christ in the USA. In that meeting, a group of members of that denomination, under the theological leadership of Gabriel Fackre of Andover-Newton Theological Seminary, attempted to define a centre, a core position which could be said to delimit the authentic Christian voice and from which one could judge, at least roughly, that some other voices are not authentically and genuinely Christian. There is, to use Fackre's terminology, a common Christian story which defines the "centre" and which can be acknowledged as distinguishing the common core of any authentic Christian voice.

The Fackres and their friends were struggling in that online meeting with what has become a common problem for most, if not all, denominations. In a time when the voices within each of our denominations are becoming increasingly diverse, what can we do about the heresies of the left and of the right which persist and even prosper within each of our communions? Can we succeed in holding on to a common centre? It is by no means certain. The pluralization of the denominations is symptomatic of this society of generalized communication which contemporary communications media have made possible. In cyberspace, then, different voices will exist side by side. It would appear that, in the age of information technology, no voice will be able to assert itself as definitive of the Christian gospel.

2. In a society of generalized communication, Christian voices exist as one among many.

We find ourselves crying in the wilderness, with no assurance, other than the number of "hits" on our Web pages, that anyone can hear. Christian voices have no special privilege. We speak on an equal footing with people of all faiths and none at all. While we can speak to all the world, so can everyone else. Any claim that we make to having a unique and ultimate word about the human condition becomes more and more problematic, more and more incredible in a situation where, de facto, no voice is privileged.

3. In a society of generalized communication, those who have formerly had no voice, who have been marginalized to the extent that they could not be heard, will be empowered to speak.

Not even the economics of communication will be an absolute bar for any voices to speak. Even the homeless can have a Web page. This is not, of course, a guarantee of equal access to the media. It is an assurance that even the voice of those who cannot afford access will speak, even if in a somewhat muted way. One of the mandates of the gospel for the church in a society of generalized communication may well be to enable the marginalized to have access to this medium so that their voice may be added to the multiplicity.

4. In a society of generalized communication, we are constantly involved in the transmission of messages.

The task of transmitting messages involves us both in the transmission of messages with our contemporaries and the transmission of messages between past and future. In a world where multiple stories exist side by side, we are involved not only in hearing each other's stories. We are forced continually to reinterpret our own in response to the multiple voices we hear.

As Christians, then, we find ourselves plunged into a world for which we are not totally unprepared, for the transmission and interpretation of messages has always been part and parcel of the life of the Christian community.

In a society of generalized communication, I would suggest, the transmission and interpretation of messages takes two forms: dialogue and witness.

The church in such a society is called to be a community that listens as well as speaks. We need to be willing to engage the multiple voices that we hear. The society of generalized communication could be a Babel in which everyone speaks but no one listens. No one attempts to understand. One of the roles of the church is to engage those voices — to listen, to understand, to challenge. That is the dialogical calling of the church.

To witness, on the other hand, cannot be construed as asserting some privilege for our own version of the Christian story. That would be an exercise in futility. In a world of multiple voices, the Christian response of witness is one of pointing to and naming the signs of the Spirit in the multitude of voices. It is the task of discerning the Spirit, of finding traces of Pentecost within the cacophony of Babel.

Select Bibliography

Jean Beaudrillard, *Simulacra and Simulation*, tr. Sheila Faria Glaser, Ann Arbor, Univ. of Michigan Press, 1994.

"Simulacra" are copies without originals. Beaudrillard's cultural analysis, emphasizing the widespread reduction of things to simulacra, is an important resource for interpreting computers and how they process "information".

Sven Birkerts, *The Gutenberg Elegies: The Fate of Reading in an Electronic Age*, New York, Faber & Faber, 1994.

A lament for the decline of the printed word in contemporary culture.

J. David Bolter, *Writing Space: The Computer in the History of Literacy*, Hillsdale NJ, Lawrence Elbaum, 1990.

An important study of the history of text and of its transformation in electronic culture.

Mark Dery, *Escape Velocity: Cyberculture at the End of the Century*, New York, Grove Press, 1996.

An authoritative study of some of the countercultures that have appeared during the past decade in response to the emergence of "cyberspace".

Donna Haraway, *Modest_Witness@Second_Millenium.Female Man©_Meets_OncoMouse™: Feminism and Technoscience*, New York and London, Routledge, 1997.

In the mid-80s, Haraway introduced the image of the cyborg as a metaphor of our human/technological identity in the late 20th century. This book continues her analysis of the cultural impact of technoscience. Haraway brings the talents of a scientist and philosopher to a feminist critique of technological culture.

Martin Heidegger, *The Question Concerning Technology and Other Essays*, tr. William Lovitt, New York, Harper & Row, 1977.

Heidegger's exploration of the "essence" of technology is a prerequisite to any reflection on its contemporary impact. His interpretation of the technological as a reduction of everything to "standing reserve" is an apt description of what computer technology does; and his enigmatic suggestion that we find in contemporary technology the coincidence of both "danger" and "saving power" well depicts the anxiety that has accompanied the appearance of digital technologies in recent years.

Kevin Kelly, *Out of Control: The Rise of Neo-Biological Civilization*, Reading MA, Addison-Wesley (Burnaby), 1994.

Kelly is editor of *Wired*, a magazine that celebrates the emerging cyberculture, and his work can be seen as a prime example of technological utopianism.

George Landow, *Hypertext: The Convergence of Critical Theory and Technology,* Baltimore, Johns Hopkins UP, 1992.
Written by a leading theorist of hypertext, this is a basic book for understanding hypertext and its impact on literary works.

Richard A. Lanham, *The Electronic Word: Democracy, Technology and the Arts,* Chicago, Univ. of Chicago Press, 1993.
Like Landow and Bolter, Lanham provides basic reflection on the importance of the recent appearance of electronic texts.

Steven Levy, *Hackers: Heroes of the Computer Revolution,* Garden City NY, Doubleday, 1984.
Levy is a journalist who has chronicled the impact of computer technology on culture. *Hackers* is a particularly illuminating study of computer culture and how computer technology has encouraged the growth of a libertarian ethic.

David Lochhead, *Theology in a Digital World,* Toronto, United Church Publishing House, 1988.
A collection of essays on computers and theology, written between 1983 and 1987. Many of the thoughts in this book were first explored in these essays.

Jean-François Lyotard, *The Post-Modern Condition: A Report on Knowledge,* tr. Geoffrey Bennington and Brian Massumi, Minneapolis, Univ. of Minnesota Press, 1984.
—, *The Postmodern Explained,* Minneapolis, Univ. of Minnesota Press, 1993.
Lyotard, a French philosopher, is a leading theorist of "postmodernism" whose work is a background for contemporary studies, like that of Sherry Turkle, on the computer as a "post-modern" technology.

Marshall McLuhan, *The Gutenberg Galaxy: The Making of Typographic Man,* Toronto, Univ. of Toronto Press, 1962.
—, *Understanding Media: The Extensions of Man,* New York, McGraw-Hill, 1964.
McLuhan's work has been praised and deplored since its appearance a generation ago. In spite of the obscurity of much of his thought, these remain basic texts for any reflection on the impact of technology on culture.

Heather Menzies, *Whose Brave New World? The Information Highway and the New Economy*, Toronto, Between the Lines, 1996.

Menzies provides an important analysis and critique of the way that new technologies are transforming the global economy.

Nicholas Negroponte, *Being Digital*, New York, Knopf, 1995.

Negroponte, director of the media laboratory at the Massachusetts Institute of Technology, is one of the most prominent and enthusiastic promoters of digital technology. In this book, he explains how digital technology is pervading our lives. It provides a good introduction to the significance of the difference between "bits" and "atoms".

Neil Postman, *Technopoly: The Surrender of Culture to Technology*, New York, Vintage, 1993.

In Postman's widely known earlier work, *Amusing Ourselves to Death*, he criticized television and its impact on our lives. Here he extends his critique to a wider indictment of contemporary technology.

Howard Rheingold, *The Virtual Community: Homesteading on the Electronic Frontier*, Reading MA, Addison-Wesley, 1993.

Rheingold, a long-time inhabitant of the online world, has written a basic text for understanding how computer communication can nourish the growth of geographically dispersed communities.

Mark Slouka, *War of the Worlds: Cyberspace and the High-Tech Assault on Reality*, New York, HarperCollins, 1995.

Slouka is another voice raised against contemporary enthusiasm for cyberspace. In Slouka's view, the new technology is a declaration of war against "reality" (that is, the physical world) in the name of a counterfeit reality produced by computer technology.

Dale Spender, *Nattering on the Net: Women, Power and Cyberspace*, North Melbourne, Spinifex Press, 1995.

Dale Spender is a feminist who confesses herself a "convert" to computer technology. In this book she offers a feminist critique of the male domination and definition of "cyberspace".

Clifford Stoll, *Silicon Snake Oil: Second Thoughts on the Information Highway,* New York, Doubleday, 1995.

Stoll made his reputation by tracking down a "hacker" in Europe who was gaining illegitimate access to sensitive computer installations in North America. His online detective work was chronicled in *The Cuckoo's Egg.* In this work, Stoll engages in what seem like random and ill-considered put-downs of digital technology, taking a position similar to that of Slouka, but Stoll's argumentation leaves much to be desired.

Allucquere Rosanne Stone, *The War of Desire and Technology at the Close of the Mechanical Age,* Cambridge MA, MIT Press, 1995.

Stone's work is important for its reflection on the relationship of the body to digital technologies.

Mark C. Taylor and Esa Saarinen, *Imagologies: Media Philosophy,* New York & London, Routledge, 1994.

Taylor is a US post-modern philosopher and theologian, Saarinen a Finnish philosopher. The two taught a course together with simultaneous classes in the United States and in Finland, mediated by state-of-the-art electronic technology. This book not only chronicles the experiment but offers important reflections on the impact of technology on thought.

Sherry Turkle, *The Second Self: Computers and the Human Spirit,* New York, Simon & Schuster, 1984.

—, *Life on the Screen: Identity in the Age of the Internet,* New York, Simon & Schuster, 1995.

Sherry Turkle's work is required reading for anyone seeking insight on how technologies affect us and the communities we form. Turkle is a social psychologist who teaches at the Massachusetts Institute of Technology.

Joseph Weizenbaum, *Computer Power and Human Reason: From Judgment to Calculation,* Harmondsworth, UK, Penguin, 1984.

In the early 1970s Weizenbaum, a computer scientist at MIT, wrote a programme named Eliza, which simulated a counselling session with a non-directive psychologist. Horrified when people took the programme seriously and actually used it for personal counselling, Weizenbaum wrote this book as a response, an attempt to distinguish human abilities from what computers do.

Risk
BOOK SERIES

The Risk Book Series from WCC Publications deals with issues of crucial importance to Christians around the world today. Each volume contains well-informed and provocative perspectives on current concerns in the ecumenical movement, written in an easy-to-read style for a general church audience.

Although any Risk book may be ordered separately, those who subscribe to the series are assured of receiving all four volumes published during the year by airmail immediately upon publication – at a substantial savings on the price for individual copies. In addition to the four new titles each year, occasional "Risk Specials" are published. Although subscribers are not automatically sent these books as part of their subscription, they are notified of their appearance and invited to purchase them under the same advantageous conditions.

If you wish to subscribe to the Risk series, please send your name and address to WCC Publications, P.O. Box 2100, 1211 Geneva 2, Switzerland. Details and an order form will be sent to you by return mail.

Some of the titles to appear recently in the Risk Book Series are:

Duncan Forrester, *The True Church and Morality: Reflections on Ecclesiology and Ethics*, 104pp.

Eva de Carvalho Chipenda, *The Visitor: An African Woman's Story of Travel and Discovery,* 96pp.

Gillian Paterson, *Love in a Time of AIDS: Women, Health and the Challenge of HIV,* 130pp.

Dafne Sabanes Plou, *Global Communication: Is There a Place for Human Dignity?,* 86pp.

S. Wesley Ariarajah, *Did I Betray the Gospel? The Letters of Paul and the Place of Women,* 72pp.